CW01083920

THE DANCE OF THE SOUL

HAZRAT INAYAT KHAN

The
Dance
of the
Soul

GAYAN VADAN NIRTAN

SUFI SAYINGS

MOTILAL BANARSIDASS PUBLISHERS
PRIVATE LIMITED ● DELHI

Reprint: Delhi, 1997, 2007
First Indian Edition: 1993

© MOTILAL BANARSIDASS PUBLISHERS PRIVATE LIMITED
All Rights Reserved

ISBN: 978-81-208-1101-0 (Cloth)
ISBN: 978-81-208-1102-7 (Paper)

MOTILAL BANARSIDASS

41 U.A. Bungalow Road, Jawahar Nagar, Delhi 110 007
8 Mahalaxmi Chamber, 22 Bhulabhai Desai Road, Mumbai 400 026
203 Royapettah High Road, Mylapore, Chennai 600 004
236, 9th Main III Block, Jayanagar, Bangalore 560 011
Sanas Plaza, 1302 Baji Rao Road, Pune 411 002
8 Camac Street, Kolkata 700 017
Ashok Rajpath, Patna 800 004
Chowk, Varanasi 221 001

Printed in India
BY JAINENDRA PRAKASH JAIN AT SHRI JAINENDRA PRESS,
A-45 NARAINA, PHASE-I, NEW DELHI 110 028
AND PUBLISHED BY NARENDRA PRAKASH JAIN FOR
MOTILAL BANARSIDASS PUBLISHERS PRIVATE LIMITED,
BUNGALOW ROAD, DELHI 110 007

CONTENTS

FOREWORD

GAYAN, VADAN and NIRTAN can be said to represent
the essence of Hazrat Inayat Khan's Sufi Message.
A musician as well as a mystic, Hazrat Inayat had
at all times a deep joy in the beauty of sound, and
his thought naturally fell into rhythmic expression.
His inspiration readily clothed itself in terms of
music. Therefore, in reading these works, we should
bear in mind that, throughout, the philosophical or
mystical idea is of the first importance, and that
there is a play upon the word 'music'. This is used
in a double sense to denote not only the rhythmic
form, but also that harmony of the divine Thought
of which such teachings are notes, faintly heard by
the soul amid the tumult of earth's many voices.
As it is said in *Gayan*, 'When the soul is attuned to
God every action becomes music'.

Hazrat Inayat speaks of manifestation as the music
of the Creator. It is out of music that the universe
was produced, and to that music every heart is
attracted; the whole of nature tells of it; and when

the heart is open, when the soul is awakened, this music becomes audible. That is why Hazrat Inayat called the first work *Gayan*, which word can best be translated by 'singing', suggesting the celestial voices, the 'unstruck music' that is the origin of all music.

Vadan, the name of the second work, is used here by Hazrat Inayat Khan in the sense of 'divine symphony', the performing of which is the purpose of creation; and in this divine symphony every soul takes a part.

In calling the third work, *Nirtan*, meaning here 'the dance of the soul', the Master wished to show that the expression of the beauty within is a mystical dance which every human being performs. When inspiration rises as a spring from the depth of the heart, when ecstasy comes through nature's song, heard as the whisper of the divine Beloved, when the light of truth manifests in joy or in tears as a pure, clear ray of God, the expression of this can be called the Dance of the Soul.

When the soul dances, every moment of life becomes a miracle; the spiritual life rises to the surface in all existing things, and one becomes living through contact with the radiant life within.

Many of the terms used for the classification of the text are those employed in Persian and Hindustani for musical or lyrical expression. The exact meaning given to each by Hazrat Inayat Khan appears below:

Alapa	Extemporization. God speaking to man; a divine word in the form of advice.
Alankara	Ornamentation. The fanciful expression of an idea.
Boula	The words of a song. A great idea in a few burning words.
Chala	Theme. An illuminated statement.
Gamaka	What comes from the heart of the poet, keyed to various notes.
Gayatri	Sacred chants. Prayers.
Raga	Modulation. The outpouring of the soul calling upon the Beloved God.
Sura	A note. God speaking through the kindled soul.
Tala	Rhythm. A rhythm formed by comparison.
Tana	Trill. The soul speaking with nature.

GAYAN

CONTENTS

ALAPAS

WHEN a glimpse of Our image is caught in man, when heaven and earth are sought in man, then what is there in the world that is not in man? If one only explores him, there is a lot in man.

If you will go forward to find Us, We will come forward to receive you.

Give Us all you have, and We shall give you all We possess.

In man We have designed Our image; in woman We have finished it.

In man We have shown Our nature benign; in woman We have expressed Our art divine.

God is the answer to every question.

Make God a reality, and God will make you the truth.

God made man, and man made good and evil.

If the Almighty God chooseth, He hath power sufficient to turn thy shield into a poisoned sword, and even thine own hand into the hand of thine adversary.

Give all you have, and take all that is given to you.

Your great enemies are those who are near and dear to you, but your still greater enemy is your own self.

Whichever path you choose, the right or the wrong, know that there is at the back always a powerful hand to help you along it.

O peace-maker, before trying to make peace throughout the world, first make peace within thyself!

Man! Thou art the master of life, here and in the hereafter.

Out of space there arose light, and by that light space became illuminated.

If your fellow-man does not pay you his debts, forbear patiently; some day every farthing will be paid you with interest.

Put thy trust in God for support, and see His hidden hand working through all sources.

ALANKARAS

INDIFFERENCE! My most intimate friend,
I am sorry I have always to act against thee as thy
opponent.

My modesty! Thou art the veil over my vanity.

My humility! Thou art the very essence of my
vanity.

Vanity! Both saint and sinner drink from thy cup.

Vanity! Thou art the fountain of wine on the earth,
where cometh the King of Heaven to drink.

Peacock! Is it not thy vanity that causeth thee to
dance?

My bare feet! Step gently on life's path, lest the

thorns lying on the way should murmur at being trampled upon by you.

My ideal! I imagine at moments that we are playing see-saw; when I rise up, thou goest down below my feet; and when I go down thou risest above my head.

My self-dependence! Thou makest me poor but at the same time rich.

My beloved ideal! When I was looking for thee on the earth, wert thou not laughing at me in heaven?

My feeling heart! I so often wish thou wert made of stone.

My limitation! Thou art as a mote in the eye of my soul.

Money! Thou art a bliss and a curse at the same time. Thou turnest friends into foes and foes into friends. Thou takest away anxiety in life and at the same time givest it.

Waves:—We are Upsaras of the ocean. When the wind plays music we dance; earth's treasure is not of our seeking; our reward is Indra's one glance.

Time! I have never seen thee, but I have heard thy steps.

Time! In my sorrow thou creepest, in my joy thou runnest; in the hours of my patient waiting thou standest still.

Time! Thou art the ocean, and every movement of life is thy wave.

Sky! Thou art a sea whereon the boat of my imagination sails.

My thoughtful self! Reproach no one, hold a grudge against no one, bear malice against no one; be wise, tolerant, considerate, polite and kind to all.

My independence! How many sacrifices I have made for thee, and yet thou art never satisfied.

My simple trust! How often thou hast disappointed me, yet I still go on following thee with closed eyes.

My moods, what are you?—We are the waves rising in your heart.

My emotion, where do you come from?—From the ever-flowing spring of your heart.

My imagination, what are you?—I am the stream that feeds the fountain of your mind.

BOULAS

HEAVEN and hell are the material manifestation of agreeable and disagreeable thoughts.

All the good deeds of a lifetime may be swept away in the flood caused by a single sin.

A learned man without will-power is like a head without a body.

All that one holds is conserved; all that one lets go is dispersed.

A pure conscience gives one the strength of lions, and by a guilty conscience even lions are turned into rabbits.

The only thing that is made through life is one's own nature.

Be either true or false, for you cannot be both.

Truth is a divine inheritance found in the depth of every human heart.

It is only out of consideration for others that the kingly soul obeys the law; otherwise he is above the law.

He who can live up to his ideal is the king of life.

The God who is intelligible to man is made by man himself, but what is beyond his intelligence is the reality.

The closer one approaches reality, the nearer one comes to unity.

A lifetime is not sufficient to learn how to live in this world.

Man looks for wonders; if he only saw how very wonderful is the heart of man!

Many evils are born of riches, but still more are bred in poverty.

Do not weep with the sad, but console them; if not, by your tears you will but water the plant of their sorrow.

The spirit of controversy is fed by argument.

Reform has a scope in every period.

When man touches the ultimate truth he realizes that there is nothing which is not in himself.

Reason is the illusion of reality.

Death is preferable to asking a favour of a small person.

Lull the devil to sleep rather than awaken him.

Movement is life; stillness is death.

There is no action in this world that can be stamped as sin or virtue; it is its relation to the particular soul that makes it so.

Reality itself is its own evidence.

It is of no use to try and prove to be what in reality you are not.

Pleasure blocks, but pain clears the way of inspiration.

A biting tongue goes deeper than the point of a bayonet, and cutting words pierce keener than a sword.

The human heart must first be melted, like metal, before it can be moulded into a desirable character.

The mystic does not wait until the hereafter, but does all he can to progress now.

Power demands subjection; but if you cannot resist power by conquest, win it by surrender.

The fountain stream of love rises in the love for an individual, but spreads and falls in universal love.

He who makes room in his heart for others, will himself find accommodation everywhere.

Each human personality is like a piece of music, having an individual tone and a rhythm of its own.

One should take oneself to task, instead of putting one's fault on another.

A tender-hearted sinner is better than a saint hardened by piety.

The way to overcome error is, first, to admit one's fault; and next, to refrain from repeating it.

The human heart is the shell in which the pearl of sincerity is found.

Rocks will open and make a way for the lover.

Man makes his reasons to suit himself.

Singleness of mind ensures success.

Love of form, progressing, culminates in love of the formless.

When man rises above the sense of duty, then duty becomes his pleasure.

The external life is but the shadow of the inner reality.

The secret of all success is strength of conviction.

Those who try to make virtues out of their faults grope further and further into darkness.

When envy develops into jealousy, the heart changes from sourness into bitterness.

A worldly loss often turns into spiritual gain.

Patient endurance is a sign of progress.

The ideal is the means, but its breaking is the goal.

Many feel, a few think, and fewer still there are who can express their thoughts.

The value of sacrifice is in willingness.

Nothing can take away joy from the man who has right understanding.

Do not fear God, but regard carefully His pleasure and displeasure.

Optimism is the result of love.

He who is a riddle to another is a puzzle to himself.

When the miser shows any generosity he celebrates it with trumpets.

A sincere man has a fragrance about him which is perceived by a sincere heart.

If you are not able to control your thought you cannot hold it.

All that detains man on his journey to the desired goal is temptation.

Fatalism is one side of the truth, not all.

Keep your goodness apart, that it may not touch your vanity.

When man denies what he owes you, then it is put on the account of God.

A refined manner with sincerity makes a living art.

The longing for vengeance is like a craving for poison.

The truly great souls become streams of love.

God is the central theme of the true poet, and the portrait which the prophets paint.

He whose love has always been reciprocated does not know the real feeling of love.

True belief is independent of reason.

Wisdom is like the horizon: the nearer you approach it the further it recedes.

When the soul is attuned to God every action becomes music.

It is the spirit of hopelessness that blocks the path of man and prevents his advancement.

The unselfish man profits by life more than the selfish, whose profit in the end proves to be a loss.

Sincerity is like a bud in the heart of man, that blossoms with the maturity of the soul.

Success is in store for the faithful, for faith ensures success.

No one will experience in life what is not meant for him.

It is not possible to be praised only and not to incur blame at any time. Praise and blame go hand in hand.

To be in uncongenial surroundings is worse than being in one's grave.

Science is born of the seed of intuition, conceived in reason.

Truth alone is success, and real success is truth.

The key to all happiness is the love of God.

By accusing another of his fault you only root him more firmly in it.

Death is a tax the soul has to pay for having had a name and a form.

Before trying to know the justice of God, one must oneself become just.

To whom the soul truly belongs, to Him in the end it returns.

In order to realize the divine perfection man must lose his imperfect self.

When the cry of the disciple has reached a certain pitch, the teacher comes to answer it.

The best way of living is to live a natural life.

Do not take the example of another as an excuse for your wrongdoing.

People who are difficult to deal with are difficult with themselves.

All situations of life are tests to bring out the real and the false.

The true seeker will never stop half-way; either he finds or he loses himself entirely.

It is sympathy rather than good food that will satisfy your guest.

The hereafter is the continuation of the same life in another sphere.

The man who is not courageous enough to take risks will accomplish nothing in life.

Not only man but even God is displeased by self-assertion.

Those who live in the presence of God look to Him for guidance at every move they make.

It is not by self-realization that man realizes God; it is by God-realization that man realizes self.

If you wish to follow in the path of saints, first learn forgiveness.

Be sparing of your words if you wish them to be powerful.

As the flower is the forerunner of the fruit, so man's childhood is the promise of his life.

The gardener uses roses in the flower-bed and thorns in making the hedge.

Love which manifests as tolerance, as forgiveness, that love it is which heals the wounds of the heart.

The greatest love in life is often that which is covered under indifference.

Indifference and independence are the two wings which enable the soul to fly.

To offend a low person is like throwing a stone in the mud and getting splashed.

The self-made man is greater than the man who depends upon another to make him.

False politeness is like imitation jewelry, and false kisses are like imitation flowers.

The unsociable person is a burden to society.

Divinity is human perfection and humanity is divine limitation.

The wise show their admiration by respect.

Many admit the truth to themselves, but few confess it to others.

It is the twist of thought that is the curl of the Beloved.

Do not accept that which you cannot return, for the balance of life is in reciprocity.

Those whom their individuality fails seek refuge in community.

Taking the path of disharmony is like entering the mouth of the dragon.

Satan comes in most beautiful garbs to hide from man's eyes his highest ideal.

Life is an opportunity, and it is a great pity if man realizes this when it is too late.

Behind us all is one spirit and one life; how then can we be happy if our neighbour is sad?

The human heart is the home of the soul, and upon this home the comfort and power of the soul depend.

Resignation is of no value except after a deed is done and cannot be undone.

Love is the Divine Mother's arms; and when those arms are outspread, every soul falls into them.

The greatest tragedy of the world is the lack of general evolution.

There is nothing that is accidental; all situations in life work towards some definite end.

Forgiveness belongs to God; it becomes the privilege of mortal man only when asked by another.

Before you can know the truth you must learn to live a true life.

Life itself becomes a scripture to the kindled soul.

Every moment of your life is more valuable than anything else in the world.

He is an unbeliever who cannot believe in himself.

Love is a weapon that can break all obstacles on one's path in life.

Self-pity is the cause of all the grievances of life.

What is given in love is beyond price.

It is our perception of time which passes, not time itself; for time is God, and God is eternal.

Man learns his first lesson of love by loving a human being; but in reality love is due to God alone.

That person becomes conqueror of life who learns to control his tongue.

Optimism comes from God, and pessimism is born of the human mind.

The mystic begins by marvelling at life, and to him it is a phenomenon at every moment.

You need not look for a saint or a master: a wise man is sufficient to guide you on your path.

The man who cannot learn his lesson from his first fault is certainly on the wrong track.

There is a pair of opposites in all things; in each thing there exists the spirit of the opposite.

A clean body reflects the purity of the soul, and is the secret of health.

It is the purity of the soul itself that gives the tendency towards cleanliness of body.

A pure life and a clean conscience are as bread and wine for the soul.

Righteousness comes from the very essence of the soul.

Reserve gives dignity to the personality; to be serious and yet gracious is the way of the wise.

When even our self does not belong to us, what else in the world can we call our own?

All things in life are materials for wisdom to work with.

Overlook the greatest fault of another, but do not partake of it in the smallest degree.

There is no source of happiness other than the heart of man.

Not until sobriety comes after the intoxication of life does man begin to wonder.

A life with a foolish companion is worse than death.

The pain of life is the price paid for the quickening of the heart.

Endurance makes things precious and men great.

The fulfilment of every activity is in its balance.

The heart of man is a temple; when its door is closed to man it is also closed to God.

Faithfulness has a fragance which is perceptible in the atmosphere of the faithful.

Spirituality is the tuning of the heart; one can obtain it neither by study, nor by piety.

A person's morality must be judged from his attitude rather than from his actions.

Right and wrong depend upon attitude and situation, not upon the action.

In the belief of every person there is some good for him; and to break that belief is like breaking his God.

Reason is a flower with a thousand petals, one covered by another.

He who does not recognize God now, will sooner or later recognize Him.

Fighting against nature is rising above nature.

Success is achieved when free-will and circumstances work hand in hand.

A sincere feeling of respect needs no words; even silence can speak of one's respectful attitude.

Simplicity of nature is the sign of saints.

The heart is the gate of God; as soon as you knock upon it, the answer comes.

Every impression of an evil nature should be met with a combative attitude.

There is no greater phenomenon than love itself.

Those guilty of the same fault unite in making a virtue out of their common sin.

Life can be full of blessings when one knows how to receive them.

Where the body goes the shadow goes also; so is truth followed by falsehood.

Life in the world is false, and its lovers revel in falsehood.

Nothing false will succeed, and if it apparently succeeds it can only bring a false benefit.

All that produces longing in the heart deprives it of its freedom.

Possibility is the nature of God, and impossibility is the limitation of man.

It is the exaltation of the spirit which is productive of all beauty.

One virtue can stand against a thousand vices.

Wickedness manifesting from an intelligent person is like a poisonous fruit springing from a fertile soil.

Failure in life does not matter; the greatest misfortune is standing still.

Consideration is born in the heart and developed in the head.

Indifference is the key to the whole secret of life.

Life is differentiated by the pairs of opposites.

There is nothing we take in this bazaar of life that we shall not sooner or later have to pay for.

A diamond must be cut before its light can shine out.

Beyond goodness is trueness, which is a divine quality.

A guilty conscience robs the will of its power.

The answer that uproots the question from its ground is truly inspired.

A jest lightens the intelligence and clears away the clouds of gloom that surround man's heart.

If man only knew what is behind his free-will he would never call it 'my will', but 'Thy Will'.

The service of God means that we each work for all.

If you wish to probe the depths of a man's character, test him with that which is his life's greatest need.

It is the lack of personal magnetism that makes a man look for magnetism in others.

Love develops into harmony, and of harmony is born beauty.

Devotion is proved by sacrifice.

It is God who, by the hand of man, designs and carries out His intended plan in nature.

As fire can cook food or burn it, so also does pain affect the human heart.

Every desire increases the power of man to accomplish his main desire, which is the purpose of every soul.

The word which is not heard is lost.

Consideration is the sign of the wise.

Faith in oneself must culminate in faith in God, for faith is a living trust.

Man's attitude is manifest in the expression of his countenance.

Happiness alone is natural and is attained by living naturally.

The mind must be one's obedient servant; when it is a master life becomes difficult.

Every experience, good or bad, is a step forward in man's evolution.

It is no use saying you know the truth; if you knew the truth you would keep silent.

The trust of the one who trusts another and does not trust himself is profitless.

Human suffering is the first call we have to answer.

Sin is the fuel for virtue's fire.

The first lesson that the seeker after truth must learn is to be true to himself.

Subtlety is the art of intelligence.

People build four walls around their ideas, lest their minds escape out of the prison bars.

It is easy to become a teacher, but difficult to become a pupil.

The soul is either raised or cast down by the effect of its own thought, speech and action.

Love rises in emotion and falls in passion.

As poison acts as nectar in some cases, so does evil.

The whole course of life is a journey from imperfection to perfection.

Every virtue is but an expression of beauty.

Every soul has its own way in life; if you wish to follow another's way, you must borrow his eyes to see it.

The answer is in the question; a question has no existence without an answer.

The one who lives in his finer feelings lives in heaven; when he puts them into words he drops down to earth.

Man's personality reflects his thoughts and deeds.

Reason is learned from the everchanging world; but wisdom comes from the essence of life.

Finding apt words to express one's thought is like shooting at a target.

A true life enables man to realize God.

The whole of life is a chemical process; and the knowledge of its chemistry helps man to make life happy.

The domain of the mystic is himself; over it he rules as king.

The water that washes the heart is the continual running of the love-stream.

The moment a person becomes straightforward a straight way opens before him.

No one can be human and not make a mistake.

A humiliated conscience dims the radiance of the countenance.

The development of one's personality is the real purpose of human life.

Man expresses his soul in everything he does.

Out of the shell of the broken heart emerges the newborn soul.

In beauty is the secret of divinity.

There is no better companion than solitude.

He who realizes the effect of his deed upon himself begins to open his outlook on life.

Life is what it is; you cannot change it, but you can change yourself.

To be alone with one's self is like being with a friend whose company will last for ever.

Speech is the sign of living; but silence is life itself.

He who keeps no secret has no depth; his heart is like a vessel turned upside down.

Wisdom is attained in the solitude.

Every desire in life has its answer; if it were not so, creation would not have gone on.

He to whom life's purpose is clear is already on the Path.

In the complete unfoldment of human nature is the fulfilment of life's purpose.

What God makes man mars; what man makes God breaks.

All things are good; but all things are not good for every person, nor right at all times.

If in truth we shall not build our hope, in what shall we build?

Life is progress, and ceasing to progress is death.

Truth is hidden in the heart of nature; therefore man naturally hides all that is precious.

The false ego is a false god; when the false god is destroyed, the true God arrives.

The lover of nature is the true worshipper of God.

One who worships God and despises man worships in vain.

We give way to our faults by being passive towards them.

When a person does not listen to us we must know it is because we ourselves do not believe.

When a defect becomes common it is considered as the normal state by the generality.

Love in its beginning lives only on reciprocity; but when fully developed it stands on its own feet.

The present spirit of humanity has commercialism as its crown and materialism as its throne.

Without humour human life is empty.

To see life as a whole is beyond the power of the generality.

All aspects of life meet and share in common in that one central point which is the divine Mind.

Patient endurance is the strongest defence.

All that is good and worth while is difficult to obtain.

The more you make of your gifts, the less becomes the value of something which is priceless.

Lack of understanding of human nature brings about all conflicts and disagreements.

The more a man explores himself, the more power he finds within.

The secret of life is balance, and the absence of balance is life's destruction.

All that is from God is for all souls.

It is not our situation in life, but our attitude towards life that makes us happy or unhappy.

Gain by the loss of another is not profitable in the end.

Speaking wisdom is much easier than living it.

Charity is the expansion of the heart.

All that is not plain is a puzzle; therefore wisdom is a puzzle to the ordinary mind.

CHALAS

THE spiritual guide performs the role of Cupid in bringing the seeking souls closer to God.

The Sufi's tendency is to look at everything from two points of view: from his own and that of another.

The true religion, to the Sufi, is the sea of truth, and all different faiths are as its waves.

The pure truth not every man can see; if he can, he needs no more teaching.

The Creator is hidden in his own creation.

Natural religion is the religion of beauty.

The same light which is fire on earth and the sun in the sky, is God in heaven.

All surrender to beauty willingly and to power un-willingly.

The creation is not only the nature of God, but also His art.

Vanity is the impetus hidden behind every impulse, that brings out both the worst and the best in man.

Time and space are but the length and breadth of the infinite.

It is presumption on the part of man when he demands in words an explanation of God.

Among a million believers in God, there is scarcely one who makes God a reality.

The God-ideal is the flower of creation, and the realization of truth is its fragrance.

A true worshipper of God sees His person in all forms, and in respecting man he respects God.

The hidden desire of the Creator is the secret of the whole creation.

Vanity is the sum total of every activity in the world.

Beauty is the object which every soul pursues.

Beauty is the life of the artist, the theme of the poet, the soul of the musician.

A charming personality is as precious as gold and as delicious as perfume.

A dancing soul shows its graceful movements in all its activities.

A charming personality is like a magnificent piece of art with life added.

Life is the principal thing to consider, and true life is the inner life, the realization of God.

The soul of Christ is the life of the universe.

The mother was the stepping-stone of Jesus to Christhood.

God speaks to the prophet in His divine tongue, and the prophet interprets it in the language of man.

The evidence of prophecy is the personality of the prophet.

The true sword of Mohammad was the charm of his personality.

As the whole of nature is made by God, so the nature of each individual is made by himself.

When the personality of an artist is absorbed in his art, it becomes art itself.

Vanity is a mask over the hidden object that attracts every soul.

Vanity is the crown of beauty, and modesty is its throne.

Without modesty beauty is dead, for modesty is the spirit of beauty.

All beauty is veiled by nature, and the greater the beauty the more it is covered.

The beauty which modesty covers, art gently uncovers; while respecting the human tendency, it unveils the beauty which human conventions hide.

Modesty is the veil over the face of the great, for God Himself is most modest, who is seen by none except those intimate with Him.

God lives in nature and is buried alive under the artificial forms which stand as His tomb, covering Him.

Nature is the very being of man, therefore he feels at one with nature.

In the country you see the glory of God; in the city you glorify His name.

True art does not take man away from nature; on the contrary, it brings him closer to her.

A good reputation is as fragile as a delicate glass.

A good reputation is a trust given to a man by other people, so it becomes his sacred duty to maintain it.

Either take good care of your reputation, or do not care for it at all.

The man who has no reputation of his own has no regard for the reputation of another.

A man without a character is as a flower without perfume.

In the sense of honour there is a divine spark hidden.

Love is the net in which hearts are caught like fish.

While everybody asks, 'Why?' of his neighbour, the mystic asks this question of himself.

The man of wealth is often merely the door-keeper of his treasure-house.

Every person inherits from his ancestors not only his body, but his mind also.

The wretched always look for some excuse to be miserable.

Man is pulled from four sides in life: by nature, circumstances, law, and the ideal.

The child born on earth is an exile from heaven.

You must never joke with a fool; if you throw a flower at him he will throw back a stone.

No tie can bind you if your heart is free.

The stilling of the heart is the true alchemy which turns mercury into silver.

In all directions of progress the ideal is the compass that shows the way.

Great personalities are few in the world, and fewer still those who know them.

No person living on earth can come up to your ideal, except some hero of a story of the past.

The one whom you expect to be your ideal will prove to be your ideal some day when he has gone past.

The true ego is born of the ashes of the false.

If by accident you step into the mud, it is not therefore necessary to keep on walking in the muddy path.

Matter is a state of spirit.

A living word is life itself.

The words that enlighten the soul are more precious than jewels.

The whole world's treasure is too small a price to pay for one word that kindles the soul.

Sympathy breaks the congestion of the heart.

A real success is proved by its durability.

An action is a reaction of thought.

Reason is the master of the unbeliever and the servant of the believer.

When a desire becomes a steady thought, its success is assured.

No sacrifice is ever too great to be offered in the cause of liberty.

Of what use is your sense, O sensible one, if it causes you to mourn over the opportunity you have lost?

Stand through life firm as a rock in the sea, undisturbed and unmoved by its ever-rising waves.

If you fail yourself, everybody will fail you.

Love climbs the mountain of life step by step.

The discovering of error is the uncovering of the light.

The truth, sincerely spoken, must certainly calm the heart of the listener.

A fruitless life is a useless life.

Gold is that which proves to be real to the end of the test.

To make God intelligible you must make a God of your own.

Truth alone can succeed; falsehood is a waste of time and a loss of energy.

What begins with deception continues and ends in deception.

The wise say in one word what the foolish cannot explain in a thousand words.

Spiritual attainment is the true purpose of every soul.

The more people you can get on with, the wiser you prove to be.

If you wish for relief in life, rise above complexity and conventionality.

It does not matter what you have lost, so long as you have not lost your soul.

One single moment of a sincere life is worth more than a thousand years of a life of falsehood.

Burning words rise from a flaming heart.

His own attitude becomes an obstacle on the path of the pessimist.

Lack of patience starves virtue to death.

Success gives an appearance of reality even to false things.

The seeming death is the real birth of the soul.

Worrying about the faults of others is an unnecessary addition to the worry we have over our own faults.

He who is the master of his own domain is the ruler of life.

To repress desire is to suppress a divine impulse.

The 'Yes' or 'No' of a reserved person has more weight and influence than a hundred words of a talkative person.

A truth that disturbs peace and harmony is worse than a lie.

No one can sustain disharmony in life, though many ignorantly maintain it.

It takes a thousand lies to prove one false statement true; but in spite of all, the lie will prove false in the end.

That person becomes a conqueror of life who learns

to control his tongue, both as to what it should say and what it should not say.

When it is difficult for the wise to judge the action of the worst sinner, who but a fool would be ready to judge a holy man?

Preaching needs art; speaking only is not sufficient; there are many who can speak the truth as a smith would hammer on the anvil.

Initiation is taking a step forward in a direction which one does not know.

Means sufficient for the simple needs of everyday life are a greater boon than the riches that add to life's struggle.

The first step in intuition is to understand the symbolical meaning of different things, and the next is to express them symbolically.

It is not a particular religion that can produce spirituality in man; spirituality depends upon the tuning of the soul.

For everything there is a time, so there comes a time for the unfoldment of the soul; but the period of that development depends upon the speed of the progress man makes through life.

In order to arrive at his ideal man must first realize his follies, and next, try to become better, believing that he can change.

All things in their beginning must be guarded from the sweeping winds of destruction, as the young plant must first be nurtured in a glasshouse.

When it is difficult even for the worldly man to live in this world, how much more difficult must it be for the spiritual one!

The ignorant believer, by his claim of belief, causes a revolt in an intelligent person, thereby turning him into an unbeliever.

A selfish person cannot imagine anyone being unselfish; therefore he always suspects the unselfish one of falsehood.

Truth is the light which illuminates the whole of life; in its light all things become clear, and their true nature manifests to view.

As water is the cleansing and purifying element in the physical world, so love performs the same service on the higher planes.

It is very difficult to evolve oneself and at the same time keep in tune with the unevolved; it is like being drawn from above and pulled from below.

God's majesty is seen in nature, but even the greatest grandeur of human life reveals Him only in miniature.

The way of the Sufi is to experience life and yet to remain above it; to live in the world and not let the world own him.

Man as a human being is capable of loving one, but his soul as the light of God is capable of loving not only the world, but even a thousand worlds; for the heart of man is larger than the whole universe.

When man has to choose between his spiritual and his material profit, then he shows whether his treasure is on earth or in heaven.

Life is an opportunity, not only of accomplishing one's desires, but of fulfilling even the deepest yearning of the soul.

Nobility of character is as inborn a quality in man as is the fragrance in the flower; it cannot be learned or taught.

It takes but a moment to drop down from heaven to earth; but for rising from earth to heaven, even a long lifetime may be insufficient.

True happiness is in the love-stream that springs from one's soul, and the man who will allow this stream to flow continually, in all conditions of life, in all situations, however difficult, will have a happiness that truly belongs to him.

A good person proud of his goodness turns his pearls into pebbles; an evil person full of remorse may make jewels of common stones.

One word of the truly inspired answers a hundred questions and avoids a thousand unnecessary words of explanation.

If you live in the vision of the past, dream on, do not open your eyes to the present. If you live in the eternal, do not worry about the morrow. But if you live for the time to come, do all you can to prepare for the future.

The bare truth alone is not sufficient; truth must be made into wisdom. And what is wisdom? Wisdom is the robe of truth.

If you walk on the path of light and yet seek the darkness, it is like being pulled by the two poles of the earth; you are torn between them, and can go in neither direction.

Love in its fullness is an inexpressible power which speaks louder than words; there is nothing that man is too weak to do when it gushes forth from his heart.

Joy and sorrow are each part of the other. If it were

not for joy, sorrow would not exist; and if it were not for sorrow, joy would not be experienced.

Man wonders about his past and future; how wonderful would life become to him if he only realized the present!

Every moment of life is an opportunity, and the greatest opportunity is to know the value of opportunity.

It is the spirit of discipleship that opens the vision; its attainment is most necessary in one's journey along the spiritual path.

When it is so very difficult to prove truth to be true, how much more difficult must it be to prove true what is false!

Purgatory is that state which mind experiences between the birth of thought and its materialization.

It is the darkness in our own heart which, falling as

a shadow on the heart of another, becomes doubt in him.

Truth conceived by the mature soul is expressed as wisdom.

Selflessness is pleasing not only to man but to God.

It is better to refuse than to accept anything unwillingly.

No love-offering can be more precious than a word or act of respect, for the highest expression of love is respect.

You must find your ideal in yourself; no ideal in life will prove lasting and true except the one you yourself make.

All that lives is spirit; and all that dies is matter.

Believe in your own ideal first if you wish others to believe in it; unless you respect your ideal yourself others will not respect it.

Power most often costs more than it is worth; the man who attains power, not knowing its proper use, loses it in the end, for all that is held by power will some day revolt.

Man proves himself to be great or small according to the importance he attaches in life to the greater or smaller things.

Goodness and wickedness both exist in human nature at the same time; only when one is manifest the other is hidden, like the lining inside the coat.

Through matter the soul attains to its highest realization; therefore the physical body is a necessity for the fulfilment of its purpose.

There is no end to reproaches; not only those at a distance or those near to one, but even the members of one's body will some day reproach one for not having received proper care and full attention.

There are many ideas which intoxicate man; many feelings act upon the soul as wine, but there is no stronger wine than selflessness.

The absence of generosity means that the doors of the heart are closed; nothing from within can come out, and nothing from without can enter in.

There is nothing on earth or in heaven which is not within the reach of man. When God is within his reach, what can be beyond it?

The seeking of every soul in this world is different, distinct, and peculiar to himself; and each can best attain the object of his search in God.

Man's individuality is proved by his wisdom and distinguished by comparison; God, being perfect, is unintelligible to man.

The expression of sentiment is an outlet for the energy of the heart, which if conserved would be a power in itself.

If a desire is not fulfilled it means that the person did not know how to desire; failure is caused by indistinctness of motive.

The personality of the prophet is the divine net in which God captures the souls drifting in the world.

A clever person with a biting tongue is like a serpent with its poisonous fang; his sarcastic remark is more hurtful than a scorpion's sting.

Let not your reputation fall into the monkeys' hands; they will look at it curiously, will mock at it, laugh at it and snatch it from each other; in the end they will tear it to pieces.

Do not entrust the devil with your secret; if you do, then he who is meant to be your slave will become your master.

Self-confidence is the true meaning of faith, and in faith is the secret of the fulfilment or non-fulfilment of every desire.

With trust in God, with good-will, self-confidence, and a hopeful attitude towards life, man will always win his battle, however difficult.

Silence in modesty speaks louder than bold words. The cracker cries aloud, 'I am the light', and is extinguished in a moment; the diamond, shining constantly, never says a word about its light.

It is not by the servility of those around him that the king is exalted; it is in the honour in which they hold him that his kingship exists.

All things existing have their opposite, except God; it is for this reason that God cannot be made intelligible.

We each create our own God, but only His form we imagine, not His life, thus making many Gods out of the one single Being.

God alone exists, whether thought of as one God or as many Gods, for all numbers are simply an extension of one.

When the human heart becomes conscious of God it becomes like the sea: it extends its waves to friend and foe.

True spirituality is not a fixed faith or belief; it is the ennobling of the soul by rising above the barriers of material life.

Truth is purifying, it is most lovable and peace-giving; but what is truth? Truth is that which cannot be spoken.

GAMAKAS

I CONSIDER myself second to none since I have realized in myself the One alone.

All things that may seem to be exalting my position, they indeed lower me in my eyes; the only thing exalting for me is the forgetting of myself entirely in the perfect vision of God.

There is nothing that I consider too good for me, or too high to attain to; on the contrary, all possible attainments seem within my reach since I have attained to the vision of my Lord.

There is nothing that I feel too humiliating for me to do; and there is no position, however exalted, that can make me prouder than I am already in the pride of my Lord.

Neither does love exalt nor hate depress me, for all

things to me seem natural. Life for me is a dream that changes continually, and when I withdraw my real self from the false, I know all things, and yet stand remote; so I rise above all changes of life.

It makes no difference to me if I am so praised that I am raised from earth to heaven, nor if I am so blamed that I am thrown from the greatest heights to the depths of the earth. Life to me is an ever-moving sea in which the waves of favour and disfavour constantly rise and fall.

To fall down does not break me or discourage me; it only enables me to rise to a still higher sphere of life.

I could not have enjoyed virtue's beauty if I had not known sin.

Every loss in life I consider as the throwing off of an old garment in order to put on a new one; and the new garment has always been better than the old.

I have learned more by my faults than by my

virtues; if I had always acted aright, I could not be human.

My intuition never fails me, but I fail whenever I do not listen to it.

Patience is the lesson I had given to me from the moment I stepped on the earth; ever since I have tried to practise it, but there is more to be learnt.

I blame no one for his wrongdoing, but neither do I encourage him in that direction.

In bringing happiness to others I feel the pleasure of God, and for my negligence I feel myself blame-worthy before Him.

Every soul stands before me as a world, and the light of my spirit falling upon it brings clearly to view all it contains.

Nothing seems either too good or too bad. I know no more distinction between saint and sinner, since I behold the one single Life manifested in all.

I consider my action towards every man as my action towards God; and the action of every person towards me I take as an action of God.

So long as I act upon my own intuition I succeed; but whenever I follow another's advice I go astray.

I work simply, not troubling about results. My satisfaction is in accomplishing the work which is given to me, to my best ability; and I leave the effects to the cause.

Life in the world is most interesting to me, but solitude away from the world is the longing of my soul.

I feel myself when I am by myself.

By respecting every person I meet I worship God, and in loving every soul on earth I feel my devotion for Him.

There is nothing in life which pleases me more than pleasing others; but it is difficult to please everyone.

I am ready to learn from those who come to teach me, and willing to teach those who wish to learn.

I regard every obstacle on my path as an incentive to a success.

I would have either heaven or hell, but not purgatory.

I do not intend to teach my fellow-men, but to show them all I see.

Hail to my exile from the Garden of Eden to the earth! If I had not fallen, I should not have had the opportunity of probing the depths of life.

At the moment when I shall be leaving this earth, it is not the number of followers which will make me proud; it is the thought that I have delivered His message to some souls that will console me, and the feeling that it helped them through life that will bring me satisfaction.

I have not come to change humanity; I have come to help it on.

If anyone strikes my heart, it does not break, but it bursts, and the flame coming out of it becomes a torch on my path.

My deep sigh rises above as a cry of the earth, and an answer comes from within as a message.

I am a tide in the sea of life, bearing towards the shore all who come within my enfoldment.

GAYATRI

SAUM

PRAISE be to Thee, Most Supreme God,
Omnipotent, Omnipresent, All-pervading,
The Only Being.
Take us in Thy Parental Arms,
Raise us from the denseness of the earth.
Thy Beauty do we worship,
To Thee do we give willing surrender,
Most Merciful and Compassionate God,
The Idealized Lord of the whole humanity.
Thee only do we worship; and towards Thee
    alone we aspire.
Open our hearts towards Thy Beauty,
Illuminate our souls with Divine Light,
O Thou, the Perfection of Love, Harmony
    and Beauty!
All-powerful Creator, Sustainer, Judge and
    Forgiver of our shortcomings,

Lord God of the East and of the West, of
the worlds above and below,
And of the seen and unseen beings,
Pour upon us Thy Love and Thy Light,
Give sustenance to our bodies, hearts and souls.
Use us for the purpose that Thy Wisdom
chooseth,
And guide us on the path of Thine Own
Goodness.
Draw us closer to Thee every moment of our
life,
Until in us be reflected Thy Grace, Thy Glory,
Thy Wisdom, Thy Joy and Thy Peace.

Amen.

SALAT

MOST gracious Lord, Master, Messiah, and
Saviour of humanity,

We greet Thee with all Humility.

Thou art the First Cause and the Last Effect,
the Divine Light and the Spirit of Guidance,
Alpha and Omega.

Thy Light is in all forms, Thy Love in all
beings: in a loving mother, in a kind father,
in an innocent child, in a helpful friend, in
an inspiring teacher.

Allow us to recognize Thee in all Thy holy
names and forms; as Rama, as Krishna, as
Shiva, as Buddha.

Let us know Thee as Abraham, as Solomon,
as Zarathushtra, as Moses, as Jesus, as
Mohammad, and in many other names and
forms, known and unknown to the world.

We adore Thy past; Thy presence deeply enlighteneth our being, and we look for Thy blessing in the future.

O Messenger, Christ, Nabi, the Rasul of God!

Thou Whose heart constantly reacheth upward, Thou comest on earth with a message, as a dove from above when Dharma decayeth, and speakest the Word that is put into Thy mouth, as the light filleth the crescent moon.

Let the star of the Divine Light shining in Thy heart be reflected in the hearts of Thy devotees.

May the Message of God reach far and wide, illuminating and making the whole humanity as one single Brotherhood in the Fatherhood of God.

Amen.

KHATUM

O THOU, Who art the Perfection of Love,
Harmony, and Beauty,
The Lord of heaven and earth,
Open our hearts, that we may hear Thy Voice,
which constantly cometh from within.
Disclose to us Thy Divine Light, which is
hidden in our souls, that we may know
and understand life better.
Most Merciful and Compassionate God, give
us Thy great Goodness;
Teach us Thy loving Forgiveness;
Raise us above the distinctions and differences
which divide men;
Send us the Peace of Thy Divine Spirit,
And unite us all in Thy Perfect Being.

Amen.

DOWA

SAVE me, my Lord, from the earthly passions and the attachments which blind mankind.

Save me, my Lord, from the temptations of power, fame, and wealth, which keep man away from Thy Glorious Vision.

Save me, my Lord, from the souls who are constantly occupied in hurting and harming their fellow-man, and who take pleasure in the pain of another.

Save me, my Lord, from the evil eye of envy and jealousy, which falleth upon Thy bountiful Gifts.

Save me, my Lord, from falling into the hands of the playful children of earth, lest they might use me in their games; they might play with me and then break me in the end, as children destroy their toys.

Save me, my Lord, from all manner of injury that cometh from the bitterness of my adversaries and from the ignorance of my loving friends. Amen.

NAYAZ

BELOVED Lord, Almighty God!
Through the rays of the sun,
Through the waves of the air,
Through the All-pervading Life in space,
Purify and revivify me, and, I pray,
Heal my body, heart, and soul.

Amen.

NAZAR

O THOU, the Sustainer of our bodies,
    hearts, and souls,
Bless all that we receive in thankfulness.

Amen.

RAGAS

THY light hath illuminated the dark chambers of my mind; Thy love is rooted in the depths of my heart; Thine own eyes are the light of my soul; Thy power worketh behind my action; Thy peace alone is my life's repose; Thy will is behind my every impulse; Thy voice is audible in the words I speak; Thine own image is my countenance. My body is but a cover over Thy soul; my life is Thy very breath, my Beloved, and my self is Thine own being.

Thou pourest wine into my empty cup wherever we meet, on hills and dales, on the tops of the high mountains, in the thick forests and in the barren deserts, on the shores of the roaring sea and on the banks of the gentle river; and there ariseth in my heart the unearthly passion and the heavenly joy.

Thou hast won my heart a thousand times over; Thou comest veiled under many and varied guises, and in every guise Thou art unique. Who is not attracted by the splendour Thou hast so skilfully produced on the face of the earth? In this beauty fair Thou shinest, adorned in myriad garbs. Thine own is all the beauty, and Thou shinest and yet art not Thyself attracted by it. Thou in this stage of life actest as friend and foe, and Thou alone seest the play performed so wonderfully. I sought Thee so long, my Beloved, and now I have found Thee at last, O Winner of my heart, and in finding Thee I have lost myself.

Let me feel Thine arms around me, my Beloved, while I am wandering away from home. Let my heart become Thy lute. Hearing Thy song my soul cometh to life. Let my virgin soul dance at Thy court, my Indra; the passion it hath is for Thee alone. O, let me lean my head on Thy breast; Thine arms enfolding me, my feet touch paradise.

Wherever I look, I see Thy beloved face, covered under many different veils. The magic power of my ever-seeking eyes lifted the veil from Thy glowing countenance, and Thy smile won my heart a thousand times over. The lustre of Thy piercing glance hath lighted my darkened soul, and lo! now I see the sunshine everywhere.

In the brightness of day and in the darkness of night what didst Thou not teach me! Thou hast taught me what is meant by wrong and what is called right. Thou hast shown me the hideous face of life, and Thou hast unveiled before me life's beautiful countenance. Thou hast taught me wisdom out of utter darkness of ignorance. Thou has taught me to think after my thoughtless moments. Thou playest with me, my Beloved Lord and Master, hide and seek! Thou closest mine eyes and Thou dost open them.

When we are face to face, Beloved, I do not know whether to call Thee me, or me Thee! I see myself when Thou art not before me; when I see Thee my self is lost to view. I consider it good fortune when Thou art alone with me, but when I am not there at all, I think it the greatest blessing.

Thy whisper to the ears of my heart moveth my soul to ecstasy. The waves of joy that rise out of my heart form a net in which Thy living Word may swing. My heart patiently awaiteth Thy Word, deaf to all that cometh from without. O Thou, who art enshrined in my heart, speak again to me; Thy voice exalteth my spirit.

When Thou art before me, my Beloved, I rise upon wings, and my burden becometh light; but when my little self riseth before my eyes I drop to earth, and all its weight falleth upon me.

My soul is moved to dance by the charm of Thy graceful movements, and my heart beateth the rhythm of Thy dancing steps. The deep impression of Thy sweet countenance, O Winner of my heart, covereth all visible things from my sight. My heart repeateth a thousand times the melody Thou playest on Thy flute; it setteth my soul in harmony with the whole universe.

I dare not think of raising mine eyes to behold Thy glorious vision; I sit quietly by the lake of my heart, watching in it Thine image reflected.

Thou givest me Thine own love and Thou winnest

my heart with the charm of Thy beauty. When I approach Thee my Beloved, Thou sayest to me, 'Touch me not'.

I cling to Thee with a child's faith, bearing Thy most lovely image in my heart. I sought refuge in Thy bosom, Beloved, and I am safe, feeling Thine arms around me.

How shall I thank Thee, my King, for Thy bountiful gifts? Every gift Thou givest me, my generous Lord, is invaluable. A tongue of flame arose from the spark in my heart by Thy gentle blowing. Thou dost hear my softest whisper; Thou hast taught me Thine own tongue and to read the character written by Thy pen.

I call Thee my King when I am conscious of my bubble-like self; but when I am conscious of Thee, my Beloved, I call Thee me.

How shall I thank Thee for Thy mercy and compassion, O King of my soul? What didst Thou not unto me when I was walking alone through the wilderness, through the darkness of night? Thou camest with Thy lighted torch and didst illuminate my path. Frozen with the coldness of the world's hardness of heart I sought refuge in Thee, and Thou didst console me with Thine endless love. I knocked at Thy gate at last when I had no answer from anywhere in the world, and Thou didst readily answer the call of my broken heart.

I searched, but I could not find Thee; I called Thee aloud, standing on the minaret; I rang the temple bell with the rising and setting of the sun; I bathed in the Ganges in vain; I came back from Ka'ba disappointed; I looked for Thee on the earth; I searched for Thee in the heaven, my Beloved, but at last I have found Thee hidden as a pearl in the shell of my heart.

I would willingly die a thousand deaths if by dying I could attain Thy most lofty presence. If it were a cup of poison Thy beloved hand offered, I would prefer that poison to the bowl of nectar. I value the dust under Thy feet, my Precious One, most of all the treasures the earth holds. If my head could touch the earth of Thy dwelling-place, I would proudly refuse Khusru's crown. I would gladly sacrifice all pleasures the earth can offer me, if I could only retain Thy pain in my feeling heart.

One moment's life lived with Thee is worth more than a life of long years lived in Thine absence.

My lifelong sorrow I forget when Thou castest Thy glance upon me. Time is not for me; one glimpse of Thy glorious vision maketh me eternal.

It is Thou who art my pride; when I realize my limited self I feel myself the humblest of all living beings.

O Thou, the seed of my life's plant, Thou wert hidden so long in my budlike soul; but now Thou hast come out, O my life's fruit, after the blossoming of my heart.

Let me grow quietly in Thy garden as a speechless plant, that some day my flowers and fruits may sing the legend of my silent past.

Thy music causeth my soul to dance; in the murmur of the wind I hear Thy flute; the waves of the sea keep the rhythm of my dancing steps. Through the whole of nature I hear Thy music played, my Beloved; my soul while dancing speaketh of its joy in song.

Thy smile has brought my dead heart to life again; my life and death depend upon the closing and disclosing of Thy magic glance.

O give me one more cup, O Saki, which I will value more than the whole life I have lived.

SURAS

BLESSED is he who has found in life his life's purpose.

Blessed is he who rests in the abode of his soul.

Blessed is he who hears the call from the minaret of his heart.

Blessed is he who sees the star of his soul as the light that is seen in the port from the sea.

Blessed are the innocent who believe and trust.

Blessed are they who patiently strive in the cause of truth and do not weary.

Blessed are they who fear lest they cause another the slightest hurt by thought, word, or deed.

Blessed are the unselfish friends and they whose motto in life is constancy.

Blessed are they who cover the scars of others even from their own sight.

Blessed are the proud in God, for they shall inherit the Kingdom of Heaven.

Blessed are they who make willing sacrifices in kindness.

Verily, the heart that cherishes the love of God will be crowned with glory on the last day.

Verily, the heart that repeats constantly the Sacred Name is exalted.

Verily, the heart that reflects the divine Light is illuminated.

Verily, the heart that is responsible to the divine Word is liberated.

Verily, the heart that receives the divine Peace is blessed.

Verily, blessing is for every soul; for every soul, whatever be his faith or belief, belongs to God.

Verily, to be envied is he who loves and asks no return.

Verily, it is truth that every soul is seeking.

Verily, the one who is hopeful will succeed in life.

Verily, life is one continual battle, and he alone is victorious who has conquered himself.

Verily, all that leads to happiness is good.

Verily the man who considers human feelings is spiritual.

Verily, the man who holds the world is greater than the world; he whom the world holds is smaller.

Spiritual attainment is attuning oneself to a higher pitch.

As the shadow is evident yet non-existent, so is evil.

It is the tongue of flame that speaks the truth, not the tongue of flesh.

Faith reaches what reason fails to touch.

There is a limit to the precautions one takes in the affairs of one's life; and the horizon of the limit is one's trust in God.

The sunglass reflects the heart of the sun; the contemplative heart reflects the divine qualities.

The period of one's spiritual development depends upon the rhythm of one's life.

All things which one seeks in God such as light, life, strength, joy and peace, these all can be found in truth.

Truth is the evidence of God; and God is the evidence of truth.

There is as much likeness between falsehood and truth as there is between the person and his shadow, the difference being that while the former has life the latter has none.

Verily, when man rises above the earth, the earth is at his feet; but when he falls beneath the earth, the earth is over his head.

Verily, the soul has no birth, no death, no beginning, no end. Sin cannot touch it, nor can virtue exalt it; it has always been and always will be, and all else is its cover like a globe over the light.

When man closes his lips God begins to speak.

There is no teacher save God; we all learn from Him.

The soul in its journey onward strikes a plane where it exclaims, 'I am the truth'.

It is preferable to all wealth we earn in life, and all friends we have attracted through life, if our conscience says at the moment when we are passing from earth, 'Thou art true'.

Spiritual attainment is to become conscious of the Perfect One, who is formed in the heart.

Self-will is the strength of the spirit; but when the false ego expresses self-will, a soul, instead of rising, falls. The spirit becomes entitled to have self-will when the soul is evolved. 'Blessed are the poor in spirit.'

TALAS

SILENCE serves as a lock on the lips of the excitable; as a barrier between two hearts severed from one another; as a shield for the wise amidst fools; as a veil over the face of the unlettered before the well-versed.

Some are masters of success and some its slaves; the one who walks through life regardless of success, him it pursues; he who pursues success, him it eludes.

Love from above is forgiveness; from below, devotion.

One who returns more good for less good, is a good man; one who returns less good for more good, is selfish; one who tries to be even in the exchange of good, is a practical person; but the one who returns good for evil is a saint.

One who returns less evil for more evil, is ordinary; one who tries to be even in returning evil, is wicked; one who returns more evil for less evil is a devil; but the one who returns evil for good, for him there is no name.

He who guards himself against being fooled by another is clever; he who does not allow another to fool him is wise; he who is fooled by another is a simpleton; but he who knowingly allows himself to be fooled shows the character of the saint.

If you wish people to obey you, you must learn to obey yourself; if you wish people to believe you, you must learn to believe yourself; if you wish people to respect you, you must learn to respect yourself; if you wish people to trust you, you must learn to trust yourself.

Man proves to be genuine by his sincerity; to be noble by his charity of heart; to be wise by his tolerance; to be great by his endurance throughout the continually jarring influences of life.

He is brave who courageously experiences all things;

he is a coward who is afraid to take a step in a new direction; he is foolish who swims with the tides of fancy and pleasure; he is wise who experiences all things, yet keeps on the path that leads him to his destination.

The warder of the prison is in a worse position than the prisoner himself; while the body of the prisoner is in captivity, the mind of the warder is in prison.

Life is a fair trade wherein all adjusts itself in time. For all you take from it, you must pay the price sooner or later. For some things you may pay in advance; for some you should pay on delivery; and for some later on, when the bill is presented.

Master is he who masters himself; teacher is he who teaches himself; governor is he who governs himself, and ruler is he who rules himself.

He who is afraid of vice is subject to vice; he who is addicted to vice is its captive; he who acquaints himself with vice is the pupil of vice; he who learns his lesson from vice, who passes through it and rises above it, is master and conqueror.

The simpleton eats more than he can assimilate; collects a greater load than he can carry; cuts the branch of the tree upon which he is sitting; and spreads thorns in his own path.

He who says, 'I cannot tolerate', shows his smallness; he who says, 'I cannot endure', shows his weakness; he who says, 'I cannot associate', shows his limitation; he who says, 'I cannot forgive', shows his imperfection.

He who has failed himself has failed all; he who has conquered himself has conquered all.

Happy is he who does good to others, and miserable is he who expects good from others.

Love that is progressive is like the sweet water of the running river, but love that does not progress is like the salt water of the sea.

There are two kinds of seekers after God: those who make Him and those who mar Him.

Every thought, speech and action that is natural, sound and loving, is virtue; that which lacks these qualities is sin.

It is foolish to be deceived by others; it is wise to see all things, to understand all things, and yet to turn the eyes from all that should be overlooked.

It is man who causes his own death; his soul is meant to live for ever.

Life is captivity, from which death is the release.

Belief in God is the fuel, love of God is the glow, and the realization of God is the flame of divine Light.

The first birth is the birth of man; the second birth is the birth of God.

What Brahma creates in years, Vishnu enjoys in a day and Shiva destroys in a moment.

Success leads to success, and failure follows failure.

It is easy to tie a knot of attachment, but it is difficult when you wish to unravel it.

Good praises good, but evil fights evil.

Fighting with another makes war, but struggling with one's self brings peace.

Snakes breed under the throne and scorpions multiply under the crown.

If you are subtle and intelligent, that is natural; but if you are simple and wise, that is a mystery.

We must forget the past, control the present, and prepare the future.

Mountains can be broken through, the ocean can be crossed, a way may be made through the air; but you cannot find a way to work with a person who is hardened in character, deep-set in his ideas, and fixed in his outlook on life.

What science cannot declare, art can suggest; what art suggests silently, poetry speaks aloud; but what poetry fails to explain in words, music can express.

He who does not miss the opportunity of doing some good is good; and he who seizes upon such an opportunity when it occurs, is better still; but he who always looks out for an opportunity for doing good, is blessed among men.

He who appeals to the human intellect will knock at the gate of the human brain: he is a speaker. He who appeals to the human emotions will enter into the hearts of men: he is a preacher. But he who penetrates the spirit of his hearers is a prophet, who will abide in their souls for ever.

Passion is the smoke, and emotion is the glow of love's fire; selflessness is the flame that illuminates the path.

He who has spent has used; he who has collected has lost; but he who has given has saved his treasure for ever.

He who knows not the truth is a child; he who is seeking truth is a youth; but he who has found truth is an old soul.

Be contented with what you possess in life; be thankful for what does not belong to you, for it is so much less care; but try to obtain what you need, and make the best of every moment of your life.

The rock can be cut and polished; hard metal can be melted and moulded; but the mind of the foolish person is most difficult to work with.

From the body of love comes reciprocity; from the heart of love comes beneficence; but from the soul of love is born renunciation.

Make your heart as soft as wax to sympathize with others; but make it hard as rock to bear the blows that fall upon it from without.

The path of freedom leads to the goal of captivity; it is the path of discipline which leads to the goal of liberty.

The present is the reflection of the past, and the future is the re-echo of the present.

Strength increases strength, and weakness brings greater weakness.

Translation is the reincarnation, and interpretation is the transmigration of the idea.

He concerns himself in vain who thinks, 'Why are not others what they ought to be?' But he who concerns himself with that he is not what he ought to be, is right.

He who fights his nature for his ideal is a saint; he who subjects his ideal to his realization of truth is the master.

To an angelic soul love means glorification; to a jinn soul love means admiration; to a human soul love means affection; to an animal soul love means passion.

He is living whose sympathy is awake, and he is dead whose heart is asleep.

What you create blindly your intelligence destroys, and what your reason creates is destroyed by your ignorance.

Man is his own example; if he be false, all is false to him, and if he be true, all is true to him.

TANAS

SUN-DEW, why is it that every insect dies
instantly when it kisses you?
— I like him so much that I devour him.
Sun-dew, where did you learn this philosophy?
— Once upon a time a voice said to me, 'I am the
love and I am the life, and whosoever cometh to
me, I embrace him and turn him into my own
being.'

Celandine, what is your meaning?
— I am a little light of the earth.

Rosebud, what didst thou do all night?
— With folded hands I was praying to heaven to
open my heart.

Water-lily, what do you represent by your white
garb?
— The purity at the heart of this lake.

Tulip, why have you opened your lips?
— To tell you what I have learned in the silence.
What did you learn?
— To make of myself an empty cup.

Orchid, what do your petals represent?
— Graceful movements of the dance.
What does your dance express?
— The earth paying homage to heaven.

Little daisies, why do you keep so close to earth?
— Because earth is the home of all mortal beings.
Little daisies, what gospel do you preach?
— Blessed are the meek, for they shall inherit the
earth.
Little daisies, for what are you here?
— To reflect heaven on earth.
Little daisies, what is your daily duty?
— To console the hearts that are trodden upon.
Little daisies, what are you doing here in the church-
yard?
— We worship God by bowing at the feet of His
creatures.

Cactus, why are you fringed with thorns?
— I am the tongue of the malicious man.
Cactus, why is your stem so thorny?
— I am the hand of the evil-doer.
Cactus, why have you thorns on your leaf also?
— I am the heart of the wicked, who take pleasure in
hurting others.

Beautiful gorse-bushes, what are you here for?
— We are little lanterns on your path.
But where do you get your prickly thorns from?
— Flowers from above, thorns from below.

Rose-bush, what are you, friend or foe?
— I am both, for my flowers are the caress of a
friend, and my thorns the sting of a foe.

Wheat-grains, why do you grow so close together?
— Unity is our strength; that is why you seek in us
your life sustenance.

Palm-tree, what do your outstretched hands signify?
— I raise my hands heavenward when I pray, and
then I pass the blessing on to the earth.

Pine-trees, what are you?

— We are the phantoms of sages who preferred vigil in the forest solitude to life in the world.

Pine-trees, what do your branches signify?

— Hands stretched out from heaven to bless the earth.

Pine-trees, for what are you made?

— We are temples erected for the worshippers of God in nature.

Pine-trees, tell me your life's secret.

— We are the shadows of souls on the cross, awaiting patiently the hour of their liberation.

Dry wood, why do they burn you?

— Because I no longer can bear fruit.

Thunderstorm, what gives you this emotion?

— My passion for the earth.

Full moon, where will you be going from here?

— Into a retreat.

Why do you take a retreat after fullness?

— To make myself an empty vessel in order to be filled again.

Church-bell, what do you repeat?
— The sacred Name of God, which resounds through my whole being.
Church-bell, what do you proclaim?
— I proclaim that every head which resounds like mine, spreads abroad the Message of God.
Church-bell, what makes you move?
— The Word of God.

Incense, what were you whispering at the church service?
— No prayer can reach God unless it arises from a glowing heart.
Incense, what did you preach at the church?
— He who endureth pain in the cause of others must rise from the mortal world to the spheres of immortality.
Incense, what does your perfume signify?
— My perfume is the evidence of my self-sacrifice.
Incense, tell me what moral is veiled in your nature?
— When my heart endures the test of fire, my hidden quality becomes manifest.
Incense, tell me the secret of your being.
— I am the heart of the lover of God, whose deep sigh rises upward, spreading its perfume all around.

Money, what do you signify?
— I am the seal of hearts; a heart once sealed by me will love no one but me.
When you leave, what becomes of your lover?
— I leave behind a mark on my lover's heart which remains always as a wound.
Money, what do you like most?
— Changing hands.
Where is your dwelling-place?
— In the heart of my worshipper.
Where do you accumulate?
— Where I am warmly welcomed.
Where do you stay?
— Where I am adored.
Money, whom do you seek?
— Him who seeks me.
Money, whom do you obey?
— Him who has risen above me; I become his slave and lie as dust at his feet.

Devil, where do you find your location?
— In doubting eyes, in a sharp tongue, in a gossip-ing mouth, in inquisitive ears, in idle hands, in restless feet, in a vicious body, in a crooked mind, in a bitter heart, and in a darkened soul.

Devil, how do you express yourself?
— In winking eyes, in sneering smiles, in cutting words and in false tears.

Why, what are you?
— I am the cry of the hungry mind.
Why, what do you signify?
— I am the knocker on a closed door.
Why, what do you represent?
— The owl which cannot see during the day.
Why, what is your complaint?
— The irritation of mind.
Why, what is your life-condition?
— I am shut up in a dark room.
Why, how long will your captivity last?
— All night long.
Why, what are you so eagerly waiting for?
— The daybreak.
Why, you are yourself the cover over the answer you want.

Match-stick, what did you say when I struck you?
— Why?

VADAN

CONTENTS

ALAPAS

IS LOVE pleasure, is love merriment? No, love is longing constantly; love is persevering unweariedly; love is hoping patiently; love is willing surrender; love is regarding constantly the pleasure and displeasure of the beloved, for love is resignation to the will of the possessor of one's heart; it is love that teaches man: Thou, not I.

Love that ends, is the shadow of love; true love is without beginning or end.

When He gives you a blow, He may give a blow even by the hand of your most loving friend; and when He caresses you, He may caress you by the hand of your bitterest enemy.

Let courage be thy sword and patience be thy shield, my soldier.

Wide space, the womb of my heart, conceive my thought, I pray, and give birth to my desire.

Every soul's longing am I; every heart hears My call; everyone feels My impulse, My friend as well as My foe.

My thoughts I have sown on the soil of your mind; My love has penetrated your heart; My word I have put into your mouth; My light has illuminated your whole being; My work I have given into your hand.

We have made all forms in order to complete the image of man.

One day I met the Lord face to face, and, bending my knees, I prayed, 'Tell me, O King of Compassion, is it Thou who punishest the sinner and givest rewards to the virtuous one?' 'No,' said He, smiling, 'the sinner attracts his punishment; the virtuous earns his reward.'

ALANKARAS

NO CLAIM, however great, can be equal to you, my mysterious self; and yet it may be you would not prove worthy of the smallest profession you made.

Unveil Thy face, Beloved, that I may behold Thy glorious vision.

Expand my heart, Lord, to the width of the sky, that the whole cosmos be reflected in my soul.

Wherever Thou shalt cast Thy glance, Beloved, a new sun will rise there.

Lift my soul, O gentle breeze, and carry it to the abode of the Beloved.

Let my heart reflect Thy light, O Lord, as in a pool of water the sun is reflected.

When I see Thy glorious vision, I am moved to ecstasy, Beloved: waves rise in my heart, and my heart turns into the sea.

O rosebud, thy blooming gives me the impression of my Beloved's countenance.

Thy invasion, Beloved, through the storm, arouses my deepest passions.

I hear, Lord, Thy speechless call in the sublimity of nature.

Light is Thy face, and shade is Thy bosom, Beloved.

Love, I do not know whether to call thee my enemy or my friend. Thou raisest me to the highest heaven, and Thou throwest me deep into the infernal region. Thou leadest me astray, and it is thou alone who guidest me on the right path. From thee, O Love, all virtues I learn, and thou art the source of all my infirmities. Love, thou art a curse and a bliss at the same time.

My heart, gather thyself together as the rose holds its petals.

Thy favourable glance causes the sun to rise in my heart, Beloved; and with the turning of Thy glance, the sun sets.

O intoxicating air coming from her dwelling-place, thou movest my soul to ecstasy.

I have loved in life and I have been loved.
I have drunk the bowl of poison from the hands of love as nectar, and have been raised above life's joy and sorrow.
My heart, aflame in love, set afire every heart that came in touch with it.
My heart has been rent and joined again;
My heart has been broken and again made whole;
My heart has been wounded and healed again;
A thousand deaths my heart has died, and thanks be to love, it lives yet.
I went through hell and saw there love's raging fire, and I entered heaven illumined with the light of love.
I wept in love and made all weep with me;
I mourned in love and pierced the hearts of men;

And when my fiery glance fell on the rocks, the
rocks burst forth as volcanoes.
The whole world sank in the flood caused by my
one tear;
With my deep sigh the earth trembled, and when
I cried aloud the name of my beloved, I shook the
throne of God in heaven.
I bowed my head low in humility, and on my
knees I begged of love,
'Disclose to me, I pray thee, O love, thy secret.'
She took me gently by my arms and lifted me
above the earth, and spoke softly in my ear,
'My dear one, thou thyself art love, art lover,
and thyself art the beloved whom thou hast
adored.'

Let the heavens be reflected in the earth, Lord,
that the earth may turn into heaven.

Let Thy word, God, become my life's expression.

Speak to me from within, my Lord; the ears of
Thy servant are listening.

My holy pilgrimage, God, is to the sacred dwelling of Thy worshipper.

Thou comest on earth, Lord, to save man, in the guise of the godly.

Speak to me, my Lord, through the words of Thy Messenger.

My heart is no longer mine, since Thou hast made it Thy dwelling-place, my Lord.

Thou wilt grant my wishes, O Knower of my heart.

O Love, I would give up throne and crown to become a slave at Thy mercy.

Let me forget myself, Lord, that I may become conscious of Thy Being.

Nature softly whispers Thy word to my ears.

I see Thine own image, Lord, in Thy creation.

It is with Thy might alone that I can lift up life's responsibilities.

In the image of man, my beloved Lord, I see Thine own countenance.

In the form of man I see the archway to Thy dwelling-place.

The heart of man is Thy sacred shrine.

Thy divine compassion radiates in fullness through the heart of the mother.

Through the loving heart of woman manifests Thy divine grace.

Nature sings to me Thy song.

O beloved ideal of my soul, pray show thyself to me in human guise.

Let me feel Thy embrace, Beloved, on all planes of existence.

My feeling heart is drawn to Thee, Lord, when Thou comest in the form of man.

It is Thy divine purity that is manifest in the innocent expression of the child.

Before whomsoever I bow, I bend before Thy throne.

In sympathizing with everyone, I offer my love to Thee, my Beloved.

Teach me, O Lord, the innocence of the child, an angel on earth.

Nature is a bridge to cross to Thy dwelling-place.

My heart, as a tree in the forest, stands patiently waiting.

Wide horizon, thou makest my heart wide as thyself.

Thou art my life and Thou art my sustenance, God.

My lips hold the prayer in them as the rosebud
holds fragrance in its heart.

Riding on the horse of hope,
Holding in my hand the rein of courage,
Clad in the armour of patience,
And the helmet of endurance on my head,
I started on my journey to the land of love.

A lance of stern faith in my hand,
And the sword of firm conviction buckled on,
With the knapsack of sincerity
And the shield of earnestness,
I advanced on the path of love.

My ears closed to the disturbing noise of the
world,
My eyes turned from all that was calling me on
the way,
My heart beating the rhythm of my ever-rising
aspiration,
And my blazing soul guiding me on the path,
I made my way through the space.

I went through the thick forests of perpetual desire,
I crossed the running rivers of longing.
I passed through the deserts of silent suffering,
I climbed the steep hills of continual strife.
Feeling ever some presence in the air, I asked, 'Are
    you there, my love?'
And a voice came to my ears, saying, 'No, still
    further am I.'

Sublime nature, thy reflection produces in my
heart God's glorious vision.

I bend towards thee, O mother earth, in veneration
of the Father in heaven.

Flowers are the footprints of Thy dancing steps.

I look up to Thee with raised head and palms
joined in worship, like the rocky mountains.

Space, I find in thee the formless God.

When I am absorbed in Thy glorious vision,
Beloved, even my tear-drops turn into stars.

Let me not be detained in the heavens, Lord, for I long impatiently to come to Thy dwelling-place.

Since my soul has caught Thy light, my glance has become a comet.

Thy divine spark in my heart is as the dewdrop in the rose; let me treasure it, Lord, as the shell preserves the pearl.

Let Thy sun shine in my heart.

Like the setting sun, I bend my head low at Thy feet, in loving surrender.

Lift the barrier, Lord, that divides Thee from me.

Thou wilt guide me aright, Lord; I am a child on life's path.

In the blooming rose I see the charm of Thy lovely countenance.

Let my faith be as firm as mountains, Lord, standing unshaken through wind and storm.

Immensity of space, thou showest to me the majesty of His presence.

Since Thy joyful smile has produced a new light in my heart, I see the sun shine everywhere.

Let my imperfect self advance towards Thy perfect Being, Lord, as the crescent rises to fullness.

Silent voice, in the stillness of night I hear thy whisper.

The gently-blowing wind kindles the fire of my heart.

When I see in Thy hand an unsheathed sword, Beloved, blood gushes out of my heart as the rising spring.

Send on humanity, Lord, the shower of Thy mercy and compassion.

My heart melts in Thy light, Beloved, as snow in the sun.

Every stem becomes Thy reed, every leaf become Thy finger, Beloved, when Thou playest Thy flute in the wilderness.

My soul, like a compass, keeps pointing to Thee, while my life is passing through the storm.

Providence, allow me to hold long life's glorious moments, I pray, for the time that is once past will never return.

Thou teachest me patience, sublime nature, by thy patient waiting.

In the light I behold Thy beauty, Beloved; through the darkness Thy mystery is revealed to my heart.

Let Thy servant, O Lord, be my Master.

Though the ever-moving life is my nature, thou art my very being, O stillness.

The light is Thy divine radiance, Beloved, and shade is the shadow of Thy beautiful self.

My life speeds towards Thee as the blowing of the wind.

Let Thy divine knowledge spread over my heart as the snow covers the mountain.

It is Thy sweetness, Beloved, which I enjoy in the sweet fragrance of the rose.

My heart has become an ocean, Beloved, since Thou hast poured Thy love into it.

Tree, you bless me by your outstretched hands.

Earth is attracted to earth; water is drawn to water; my soul yearns to be in Thy bosom, Beloved, in the wide space.

I hear Thy whisper, Beloved, in the morning breeze.

Dig my heart, Beloved, and Thou wilt find in its depth the spring of Thy love.

My soul is Thy spirit, Master, now that I exist no more.

It is Thee, Beloved, whom I see in all names and forms.

Thou art closer to me than my self.

Let Thy might strengthen me, Thy light inspire me, Lord, and Thy love move my soul to the ultimate joy.

My life is running towards Thee, O divine Ocean, as the river flows to the sea.

Rose, in thy petals I see the rosy cheeks of my Beloved.

Make me lose myself, Lord, in Thy vision.

Let every moment of life whisper Thy name to my ears.

Thou blowest the fire of my heart, Beloved, by fanning it with the fluttering leaves.

Light is Thine eye, Beloved, and shade is its pupil.

Be Thou before me, Lord, when I am awake, and within me when I am asleep.

In my veneration for the aged I worship Thee, O God.

I drink the wine of Thy divine presence and lose myself in its intoxication.

Let my soul reflect, Beloved, the beauty of Thy colour and form.

Let my heart bloom in Thy love as the rose.

As invisible as space, as inconceivable as time, is Thy being, O Lord.

Teach me, Lord, to tread upon the sea of life.

Even the branches swing in ecstasy when they receive Thy message.

Sublime nature, let my heart find rest in thy stillness.

In the light Thou art manifest, God; in the shade Thou art hidden.

One more cup, Beloved, that I may entirely lose myself.

I see the Beloved's beauty in all colours and in all forms.

Flowers speak to me of Thy loveliness, and tell me how beautiful Thou art.

Fill my heart with Thy divine beauty as Thou fillest space with the splendour of Thy wonderful creation.

Heaven has Thy light and the earth Thy shade.

Gentle breeze, thy touch to me is the caress of the Beloved.

Let me rise towards Thee with the rising of the sun.

The sun sets, the moon wanes, the spring passes, the year ends. I asked of life, 'Tell me, how long will you continue to be?' 'I?' said life, 'I shall live for ever.'

Blowing wind, carry my message, I pray, to the dwelling-place of the divine Beloved.

We shall see who will endure to the end, my persevering adversary or I with my long-cherished patience.

The waves of the sea, even as I, rise with out-stretched hands to reach Thee, Lord, and fall at Thy feet in ecstasy.

O nature sublime, pregnant with divine spirit, thou speakest the prayer that rises from my heart.

Let my heart reflect Thy divine light, Lord, as the moon reflects the light of the sun.

Happiness, certainly thou didst play hide-and-seek with me; since I have been in thy pursuit, I saw in the world thy shadow cast, and in paradise I saw thy reflection; in pleasure I saw a veil over thy beautiful countenance, in pain I saw the dust lying beneath thy feet.

My intuition, hast thou ever deceived me? No, never. It is my reason which so often deludes me, for it comes from without; thou art rooted within my heart.

Let me be melted in Thy divine ocean as a pearl in wine.

Alone on the sea, alone on land. In the crowd and in solitude, alone I stand.

My considerate self, seek not pleasure through the pain of another, life through the death of another, gain through the loss of another, nor honour through the humiliation of another.

Let my heart become the spring of Thine infinite life, rising for ever and ever.

I see Thy mystery hidden, Beloved, under the petals of the flower.

My heart, hold closely the oil which keeps the light burning.

Pain, my life-long comrade, if all went and left me, you would still be there.

With the opening and closing of Thine eyes, Beloved, the sun rises and sets in my heart.

My self, how wonderful it is to feel that if no one in the world understood me, still you would understand.

My heart is moved to tears by thy swift moving, O gentle air.

Those who are given liberty by Him to act freely, are nailed on the earth; and those who are free to act as they choose on the earth, will be nailed in the heavens.

My sense of shame, did I not uphold thine honour, standing assaulted by the onslaught from every side?

The blowing rose brings to me Thy perfume, Beloved, which moves my heart to ecstasy.

Raise me, Lord; let me not be drowned in the sea of mortality.

Speak, Lord, in the stillness of nature; my heart's ears are open to hear Thy call.

My endurance, thou hast crushed me until I became thy clay kneaded to make a body for the divine Spirit to dwell in.

O nature sublime, in thy silence I hear thy mournful cry.

Ever-moving sea of life, am I not but a wave rising in thy heart?

Thanks to the winner of my heart, there is nothing
of me left any more.

My thoughtful self,
Bear all and do nothing,
Hear all and say nothing,
Give all and take nothing,
Serve all and be nothing.

While I was roaming through the forest, a thorn
pricked my bare foot and cried, 'Ah, you have
crushed me.' I felt sorry and I asked its forgiveness.

A wasp flying in the air stung my arm and
cried, 'Ah, you have caught me in your sleeve.'
I felt sorry and I asked its forgiveness.

My foot slipped and I fell in a pool of muddy
water. The water cried, 'Ah, you have disturbed
me.' I felt sorry and I asked its forgiveness.

I absently happened to touch a burning fire, and
the fire cried, 'Ah, you have extinguished me.' I
felt sorry and I asked its forgiveness.

I asked my gentle self, 'Have you received any
harm?' 'Be thankful,' said she, 'that it was not
worse.'

I will soar higher than the highest heaven,
I will dive deeper than the depths of the ocean,
I will reach further than the wide horizon,
I will enter within my innermost being.
You know me but little, O everchanging life,
I will live in that sphere where death cannot reach.
I will raise my head high before you will turn
  your back to me,
I will close my lips before you will close the doors
  of your heart,
I will dry my tears before you will not respond to
  my sigh,
I will fly to the heavens, O world of illusion, before
  you will throw me down on the earth.

Golden Rules

My conscientious self:

Keep to your principles in prosperity as well as in adversity.

Be firm in faith through life's tests and trials.

Guard the secrets of friends as your most sacred trust.

Observe constancy in love.

Break not your word of honour whatever may befall.
Meet the world with smiles in all conditions of life.
When you possess something, think of the one who does not possess it.
Uphold your honour at any cost.
Hold your ideal high in all circumstances.
Do not neglect those who depend upon you.

SILVER RULES

My conscientious self:
Consider duty as sacred as religion.
Use tact on all occasions.
Place people rightly in your estimation.
Be no more to anyone than you are expected to be.
Have regard for the feelings of every soul.
Do not challenge anyone who is not your equal.
Do not make a show of your generosity.
Do not ask a favour of those who will not grant it you.
Meet your shortcomings with a sword of self-respect.
Let not your spirit be humbled in adversity.

COPPER RULES

My conscientious self:
Consider your responsibility sacred.
Be polite to all.
Do nothing which will make your conscience feel guilty.
Extend your help willingly to those in need.
Do not look down upon the one who looks up to you.
Judge not another by your own law.
Bear no malice against your worst enemy.
Influence no one to do wrong.
Be prejudiced against no one.
Prove trustworthy in all your dealings.

IRON RULES

My conscientious self:
Make no false claims.
Speak not against others in their absence.
Do not take advantage of a person's ignorance.
Do not boast of your good deeds.
Do not claim that which belongs to another.

Do not reproach others, making them firm in their faults.

Do not spare yourself in the work which you must accomplish.

Render your services faithfully to all who require them.

Seek not profit by putting someone in straits.

Harm no one for your own benefit.

SURAS

VERILY, the domain of every soul is in his own sphere.

Verily, he in whose heart my star shines is blessed.

Verily, the man who lives religion through his life in the world is pious.

Verily, every atom sets in motion each atom of the universe.

Verily, in man is reflected all that is in heaven and on earth.

Verily, the power of the word can move mountains.

Verily, the one who knows the influence of time knows the secret of life.

Verily, man is his own mind.

Verily, spirit has all the power there is.

When He gives His bountiful gifts, He may give by the hand of your worst enemy; and when He takes all you possess, He make take it away even by the hand of your best friend.

Death takes away the weariness of life, and the soul begins life anew.

Death is a sleep from which the soul awakes in the hereafter.

Death is the crucifixion after which follows the resurrection.

Death is the night after which the day begins.

It is death which dies, not life.

The life everlasting is hidden in the heart of death.

RAGAS

BELOVED, Thou makest me fuller every day.
Thou diggest into my heart deeper than the depths
of the earth.

Thou raisest my soul higher than the highest
heaven, making me more empty every day and
yet fuller.

Thou makest me wider than the ends of the
world; Thou stretchest my two arms across the
land and the sea, giving into my enfoldment the
East and the West.

Thou changest my flesh into fertile soil; Thou
turnest my blood into streams of water; Thou
kneadest my clay, I know, to make a new
universe.

In the swinging of the branches, in the flying of the
birds, and in the running of the water, Beloved,
I see Thy waving hand, bidding me good-bye.

In the cooing of the wind, in the roaring of the
sea, and in the crashing of the thunder, Beloved,
I see Thee weep and I hear Thy cry.

In the promise of the dawn, in the breaking of the
morn, in the smiles of the rose, Beloved, I see
Thy joy at my homecoming.

Let Thy wish become my desire,
    Let Thy will become my deed,
Let Thy word become my speech, Beloved,
    And Thy love become my creed.

Let my plant bring forth Thy flowers,
    Let my fruits produce Thy seed,
Let my heart become Thy lute, Beloved,
    And my body Thy flute of reed.

When I close my eyes in the solitude, I see Thy
glorious vision in my heart, and, opening my
eyes amidst the crowd, I see Thee acting on the
stage of the earth. Always I am in Thy dazzling

presence, my Beloved; Thou takest me to heaven, and Thou bringest me on earth in the twinkling of an eye.

Let me not fall low after having raised me high; let me not become narrow after having made me broad. Let me not become small after having once made me great; throw me not down, Beloved, after once Thou hast lifted me up.

I looked and looked, to find someone to whom I might give my trust; but I found no one, until I saw Thee at last in my heart, holding in Thy hand the record of my life's secret.

As I put myself forward into the world, so I show my limitation, my King; but as I withdraw myself from the world, so I enter into Thy Kingdom.

I look to Thee, O Lord, when the noose of death
$$\text{seems unavoidable and}$$
$$\text{nigh.}$$

I look to Thee, O Lord, when with heavy heart
I see my beloved ones
depart.

I look to Thee, O Lord, when change and limit
in the worldly love I
see.

I look to Thee, O Lord, when all that I call mine is
snatched away from
my hand.

I look to Thee, O Lord, when my boon com-
panions turn their back
in my sorrow.

I look to Thee, O Lord, when my hands are full
with worldly strife.

I look to Thee, O Lord, when the higher self
raises me up and the
lower self weighs me
down.

I look to Thee, O Lord, when I try to do right
and it turns to wrong.

I look to Thee, O Lord, when all in life seems as
naught to me and I
feel a yearning for
something beyond.

The spring that rises out of my heart Thou pourest upon me, my Beloved, and my spirit feels the exaltation of being dissolved under Thy divine shower.

When Thou didst sit upon Thy throne, with a crown upon Thy head, I did prostrate myself upon the ground and called Thee my Lord.
When Thou didst stretch out Thy hands in blessing over me, I knelt and called Thee my Master.
When Thou didst raise me from the ground, holding me with Thine arms, I drew closer to Thee and called Thee my Beloved.
But when Thy caressing hands held my head next to Thy glowing heart and Thou didst kiss me, I smiled and called Thee myself.

What I may not see, let me not see;
What I may not hear, let me not hear;
What I may not know, I ask not to know.
Beloved, I am contented with both Thy speech and Thy silence.

Let him not see me who should not see me;
Let him not hear me who will not hear me;
Let him not know me who need not know me.
Beloved, veil and unveil me as Thy wisdom
chooseth.

By Thy skilful hands Thou hast made these flowers;
by the power of Thy magic glance Thou hast
coloured them so beautifully: Thou hast breathed
on flowers, giving them life and radiance, and with
a kiss Thou hast made them fragrant.

Let my insight be deeper than the ocean; let my
mind be more fertile than the land; let my heart be
wider than the horizon, Beloved; and let my soul
soar higher than Paradise.

Every form I see is Thine own form, my Lord,
And every sound I hear is Thine own voice;
In the perfume of flowers I perceive the fragrance
of Thy spirit;
In every word spoken to me I hear Thy voice, my
Lord.

All that touches me is Thine own touch;
In everything I taste I enjoy the savour of Thy
    delicious spirit.
In every place I feel Thy presence, Beloved;
In every word that falls on my ears I hear Thy
    message.
Every thing that touches me, thrills me with the
    joy of Thy kiss;
Wherever I roam, I meet Thee; wherever I reach,
    I find Thee, my Lord;
Wherever I look, I see Thy glorious vision; what-
    ever I touch, I touch Thy beloved hand.
Whomsoever I see, I see Thee in his soul;
Whoever aught gives to me, I take it from Thee.
To whomsoever I give, I humbly offer it to Thee,
    Lord;
Whoever comes to me, it is Thou who comest;
On whomsoever I call, I call on Thee.

Turn me not aside, Beloved, once Thou hast
granted me Thy favour; starve me not of a kiss,
after Thou hast enfolded me; grieve me not,
Beloved, since Thou hast made me smile; turn
not away Thine eyes, once Thou hast poured the
wine of Thy magic glance into the cup of my heart.

Enter unhesitatingly, Beloved, for in this abode
there is naught but my longing for Thee.
Do I call Thee my soul? But Thou art my spirit.
Can I call Thee my life? But Thou livest for ever.
May I call Thee my Beloved? But Thou art Love
itself.
Then what must I call Thee? I must call Thee
myself.

Why did I not recognize Thee when first I opened
my eyes on the earth?
Why did I not respond to Thee when I heard Thy
enchanting voice?
Why did I not feel Thy gentle hand when Thou
didst caress my face?
Why did I not cling to Thee, Beloved, when
Thou lovingly didst kiss my lips?
When I began to look for Thee, in the twinkling
of an eye Thou didst disappear.
When I started in Thy pursuit, Thou didst move
away from me still farther.
When I called Thee aloud in my distress, Thou
didst not hear my soul's bitter cry.
Cross-legged I sat in silence; then alone I heard
Thy call.

Why have I two eyes if not to behold Thy glorious
vision?
Why have I two ears if not to hear Thy gentle
whisper?
Why have I the sense of smell if not to breathe
the essence of Thy spirit?
Why have I two lips, Beloved, if not to kiss Thy
beautiful countenance?
Why have I two hands if not to work in Thy
divine cause?
Why have I two legs if not to walk in Thy spiritual
path?
Why have I a voice if not to sing Thy celestial
song?
Why have I a heart, Beloved, if not to make it
Thy sacred dwelling?

Did I not leave the unseen world in Thy pursuit?
Have I not come to this world of limitations in
search of Thee?
Have I not followed Thy footprints on this earth?
Have I not looked for Thy light in the heavens?
But where did I find Thee, Beloved, at last?
Hiding in my heart.

Every step in Thy path draws me nearer to Thee, every breath in Thy thought exhilarates my spirit, every glimpse of Thy smile is inspiring to my soul, every tear in Thy love, Beloved, exalts my being.

TANAS

LITTLE dandelions, what are you doing here?
— We reflect on earth the stars in the heavens.

Little pool, why is your water so muddy?
— Because of my narrow mind and depthless heart.

Coal, what makes you so black?
— I am the evil of the ages accumulated in the heart of the earth.
What is your penalty?
— I must pass through a trial by fire.
What becomes of you in the end?
— I turn into a diamond.

Earth, to the clouds:—Why did you come back after once you had deserted me?
— The heavens would not have us before we had reconciled ourselves with you.

Little rosebud, what do you hold between your hands?
— The secret of my beauty.

Sunflower, what are you?
— I am the eye of the seeker who searches for the light.

Death, what are you?
— I am the shadow of life.
Death, of what are you born?
— I am born of ignorance.
Death, where is your abode?
— My abode is in the mind of illusion.
Death, do you ever die?
— Yes, when pierced by the arrow of the seer's glance.
Death, whom do you draw near to you?
— I draw him closer who is attracted to me.
Death, whom do you love?
— I love him who longs for me.
Death, whom do you attend?
— I readily attend him who calls on me.
Death, whom do you frighten?
— I frighten the one who is not familiar with me.

Death, whom do you caress?
— The one who lies trustfully in my arms.
Death, with whom are you severe?
— I am severe with him who does not readily
respond to my call.
Death, whom do you serve?
— I serve the godly, and when he returns home I
carry his baggage.

Boat:—I take you in my bosom on the water.
Waggon:—I carry you on my back on the land.

Roseflower, why are your lips drooping?
— I am thinking over my glorious past.

Why do you rise, wave, with the coming of the
wind?
— To receive the message it brings.

Moth:—I gave you my life.
Flame:—I allowed you to kiss me.

Sea, why is your colour blue?
— It is heaven reflected in my white heart.

Earth, tell me your moral principle.
— I lay myself before those who pass over me, and those who come unto me, to them I open my heart.

Night, why do you cry so mournfully?
— I cry over the loving souls whom life has thrown apart, and those whom destiny will separate one day.
Night, why are you so dark?
— Light has left me.

Night, what makes you so beautiful?
— The coming of the moon, which has brought me wisdom's message.

Wind, what makes the sea respond to you so whole-heartedly?
— In her I have touched her deepest chord.
Wind, what have you done to thrill the whole being of the sea to passion?
— Nothing, only given a kiss.

'So' gives rise to an argument; 'Why?' continues it; and it ends in 'No'.

What sense is there, O moth, in burning yourself in trying to kiss the light?
— My joy in it is greater than my sacrifice.

Waves, why does the wind come and then go from you?
— It comes to wake us, and leaves us to solve the problem among ourselves.

Moving waves, the wind has left you and you are still in commotion.
— We are still repeating the word it has taught us; it moves our whole being to ecstasy.
Waves, why do you all become excited and then all calm together?
— Because behind our individual action there is one impulse working.
Rising waves, what motive is behind your impulse?
— The desire to reach upwards.

Sea, what is it that makes you so chaotic?
— No sooner does the air whisper to my ears the message of wisdom, than an enormous trouble begins within myself.

Storm, you invade us suddenly without any warning!
— I send my ultimatum by the hand of the wind, before starting gunfire.
Storm, why are the clouds being scattered now?
— I have given orders for demobilisation.
Storm, why do you send the rain after you have gone?
— To make peace with the earth.

Man:—Devil, will you be my friend?
Devil:—I am at your disposal.

Waves:—Do we not lay ourselves in complete surrender before you for you to pass over us? Then listen to our request: throw into the water those you carry in your bosom.
Boat:—No, I am not like you who drown beneath your feet those who seek refuge in your arms. The ones whom I hold in my heart, either I sink with them or I carry them safely to their destination.

Earthly riches, explain to me your character.
— I fly from the hand that holds me, I escape from the one who pursues me, I fall into his purse

who collects me, I live with him who spares me, I leave the one who does not look after me, I keep away from him who has me not. The one who does not possess me is poor indeed, but the one who possesses me is poorer still.

GAMAKAS

I WOULD rather have a lasting pain than a pleasure that passes away.

My mind never changes, but I change my mind whenever I wish.

My soul often has the feeling of being stretched, held fast by the heavens and pulled continually by the earth.

My errors do not lull me to sleep, but they open my eyes to a deeper vision of life.

My smallest work in the inner plane is worth more than all I do in the outer world.

No sooner is my heart struck than a switch is turned and the light appears.

All that I can manage in life, I take as my responsibility, but all that I cannot manage, I leave to God.

When I try to do some good to the others, I never think it is enough; but when I receive the slightest good from others, I feel it is more than sufficient.

When I open my eyes to the outer world I feel myself as a drop in the sea; but when I close my eyes and look within, I see the whole universe as a bubble raised in the ocean of my heart.

How did I rise above narrowness? The edges of my own walls began to hurt my elbows.

I would die proud rather than live a long life of humiliation.

All that is done and cannot be helped, I leave to fate; but I feel myself responsible for all that is to be done.

The scriptures have called Him the Creator; the Masons have called Him the Architect; but I know Him as the Actor on this stage of life.

I respect all those of great names, but seek continually the nameless.

I am resigned to the past, attentive to the present, and hopeful for the future.

I accept no refusal from the heavens.

Christ—His image in the church, His spirit in my soul.

I have not come to teach what you know not; I have come to deepen in you that wisdom which is yours already.

He who has lost me, is lost; he who has found me, has found life eternal.

My presence stimulates in your heart that feeling which must always be kept alive.

Be not disappointed if I tell you about things which are already known to you. Realize that they can never be repeated too many times.

There is nothing too good or too bad for me, since I am conscious of that reality which is hidden and yet covers all.

I am what I am; by trying to be something, I make that self limited who in reality is all.

I do not give you my ideas; what I give you is my personal knowledge.

My heart is the key to the hearts of men.

I need remove no one to place another in my heart; my heart is large enough to accommodate each and all.

I learn from my mureeds more than they learn from me.

I neither defend the wrongdoer nor do I condemn him.

I try to do the right which seems right to me at the moment; at another moment the same may seem to me wrong. Therefore I do not attempt to impose my right upon the one who does not see the right of it.

Nothing new I say when I speak; I only renew the memory of things which may not be forgotten.

I play my melody while everyone sings his own song.

My friends lull me to sleep, but my enemies keep me awake.

Praise fans the glow of my heart, and blame turns it into a blaze.

What has happened, has happened; what I am going through, I shall rise above; and what will come, I will meet with courage.

While I am working, I learn something; while I am thinking, I discern something; while I am speaking, I teach something; while I am silent, I reach something.

Art is dear to my heart, but nature is near to my soul.

If I were not as I am, I would not have been what I am.

When I open my eyes and look at the wide world I become great; when I close my eyes and look within, I become greater still.

BOULAS

A VIRTUE carried too far may become a sin.

At the end of the valley of sin, do not be surprised if you find virtue standing.

Souls unite at the meeting of a glance.

Success spoils people, failure ruins them.

Things are as you look at them.

One who is never alone does not know the joy of being alone.

The heart which is not struck by the sweet smiles of an infant is still asleep.

Belief is a conception, but faith is conviction.

To love is a sin, and not to love is a crime.

When facts fall dead, truth comes to life.

Nothing matters really, though everything matters.

Neither fight evil nor embrace it; simply rise above it.

The pursuit after truth is more interesting than its attainment.

When one has risen above human love, divine love springs forth.

Shatter your ideals upon the rock of truth.

Let your virtues dissolve in the sea of purity.

Make your doctrines fuel for the higher intelligence.

You need not trust the one whom you do not know, so long as you do not distrust him.

It is easy to be just, but difficult to be wise.

If you will not rise above the things of this world, they will rise above you.

Even the wisest man must sometimes stray from wisdom.

Too much enthusiasm pushes the object of attainment farther off.

Anxiety paralyses activity.

Worry consumes the spirit of action.

Even with God one can find fault. But where is the fault? In the person who finds it.

The load of responsibility weighs upon a soul more than the strain of work.

Perfection forgives, and limitation judges.

A home is made and a house is built.

Do not let your heart offer anyone such food as will increase his appetite and decrease your fund of supply.

Make the snake your friend rather than your enemy.

All men are equal in truth, not in fact.

What limits God? His name.

Life is too small a price to offer to someone whom you really love.

The real learning is unlearning all that one has learned.

To judge man, God borrows from man his sense of justice.

To investigate the wrongdoing of someone is like digging deep into the mud.

Prayer is a deep-felt need of the soul.

Man sees the right side of his own mind and the wrong side of another's.

What enables man to earn a good name? Shame.

Put your theories in practice before you expound them.

First believe in the God who is all-exclusive, and then realize the God who is all-inclusive.

As pleasure is the shadow of happiness, so fact is the shadow of truth.

Fact is to be observed in action and truth in realization.

Usually, in everything man says and does, he denies reality.

Fact is a covering over truth.

Fact or no fact, truth proves and disproves all.

Jealousy is the refuse of the heart.

Pity the wicked one for his evildoing, for he can do no better.

Woman is a stepping-stone to God's sacred altar.

If there is any place where one can meet with God, it is this earth-plane.

Righteousness is nothing but a natural outcome of right thinking.

Every action that defeats its own object is wrong.

No creature in the world is as attractive and as repellent as man.

Simplicity is the living beauty.

If you do not want to understand, you will not understand.

The man who will not take in the idea of unity, will be taken in by unity some day.

There is no use arguing, 'Have you done wrong or have I done wrong?'; all that need be done is to right the wrong.

Life offers opportunity either to pick up pearls and throw away pebbles, or to pick up pebbles and throw away pearls.

The mystic retains something of childhood all through his life.

The realization of truth is the greatest luxury.

Fact is the illusion of truth.

Woman is woman, whether in the East or in the West.

Shadow is the shadow of shadow, not of light; the ego is light itself, and so it has no shadow.

The false ego is the shadow of the body seen in the sky, not the reflection of the soul.

Heart talks to heart, soul speaks to soul.

Truth is not acquired but discovered.

Nature regards no conventionality.

You cannot be too wise, but you can be too clever.

A bitter taste lasts only as long as it is in the mouth.

Carry as heavy a load as you are able to carry easily.

If your heart is large enough, there is nothing it will not accommodate.

By calling him by his name you will raise Satan from his grave.

We cannot appreciate another's kindness if we think of all the good we have done to the other.

There is no greater teacher for the evildoer than evil itself.

Devotion without wisdom is like salt water.

What were the great personalities whose light has shone upon millions of people? Examples.

The claim of Christhood seemed too great for Jesus in the eyes of men; therefore he was crucified by the intolerant world.

Thought and feeling often take opposite directions.

Do not enjoy life more than life allows you to enjoy it; if so, your joy will turn into sorrow.

Hierarchy is the Sufi's way, but equality of all men is his truth.

Man rises above sins, but not above the reproaches of those who witness.

The clever man knows best how to tell a lie, the wise man knows best how to avoid it.

Approach woman gently, lest you jar upon her tender feelings.

God is God and man is man, yet God is man and man is God.

Peace-making is much more difficult than war-making.

It is the dead who cause death, the living preserve life.

You cannot live truth; you can realize it.

Wrong is wrong from the beginning to the end, and right is right from the first to the last.

Evil brings success to the wicked, and virtue wins victory for the righteous.

Faults and merits both serve as steps to those who go up as well as to those who go down.

It is more difficult to tame man than a lion.

Reason not with those who are incapable of understanding your reason.

Politeness in words and politeness in deeds are two different things.

No one may claim perfection, though everyone may strive after it.

You need not do something today because you did it yesterday.

Cupidity must be renounced, not joy.

The burning fire of hell does not consume the sinner; it only consumes his sins.

Wisdom is the way in which to express life as one has understood it oneself.

Man learns to follow the will of God by practising self-denial.

Man who is infallible cannot be superhuman; he may be inhuman.

Evil doings apart, evil intentions bring about disastrous results.

The knowledge of plurality begins life; but in the consciousness of unity is life's culmination.

Faith reaches beyond the limit of human comprehension.

It is the optimist who takes the initiative: the pessimist follows him.

Morality is a flower which springs out of the plant of individuality.

True piety is sincerity.

Principles are to guide one's life, not to restrict it.

Love that is free from attachment is the love of sages.

The right attitude in life is to keep a balance between justice and kindness.

The presence of the Holy One is the sacred river.

It is better not to do than to do things badly.

To analyze love is to destroy love.

Subtle ideas are best expressed simply.

Every body reincarnates, not every soul.

If you say, 'I cannot', you will not; if you will, you can.

Love that endureth not, is heart's illusion.

When optimism is exhausted, pessimism springs up.

Indeed, a virtuous woman shows divine purity.

Coming into the presence of the godly, is like entering into the gate of God.

In the union of two loving hearts is the Unity of God.

The sin of the virtuous is a virtue, the virtue of the sinner is a sin.

The shade adds to the light, as zero adds to the figure.

The heart of the Holy One is the gate of God's shrine.

Love has its own law.

Beauty is finished in simplicity.

In the spirit of duty there is the soul of religion.

What is rooted out in the quest of truth, is ignorance.

Balance is the keynote of spiritual attainment.

Beauty is not power but the possessor of it.

Do not fall in love but rise.

What may give vanity to one, may give shame to another.

Great people have great faults, but their greatness is their greatest fault.

Nothing that your mind can conceive, does not exist.

Life teaches one more than all the teachings in the world.

An experience gained as late as the last hour of one's life, is still a gain.

Nothing is lost as long as your hope is not lost.

All will help you if you will help yourself.

Astonishment is nothing but an expression of one's ignorance.

Leave all that unsaid which, by being said, creates inharmony.

Many say they tell the truth, but few there are who know the truth.

The mystic does not possess knowledge, for he is knowledge himself.

The mystic does not observe the law; he himself is the law.

A great gift and no virtue is like a flower without fragrance.

Pleasures cost more than they are worth.

Patient endurance crowns goodness with beauty.

A bad nature is the worst immorality.

One who is understood, is beneath the one who understands him.

Passion is but another form of love.

Recognize a mystic, not from what he does, but from what he is.

Shameless is lifeless.

By rising above facts, we touch reality.

It is our words that hide reality.

Outward things matter little; it is inward realization which is necessary.

Every failure follows upon a weakness somewhere.

He who cannot help himself, cannot help others.

The wrong use of every good thing is bad; the right use of every bad thing is good.

Hatred brings hatred; love brings love.

If you begin from the end, you will finally arrive at the beginning.

Beware lest your remedy become your malady.

Will is not a power, but all the power there is.

What is God? God is what is wanting to complete oneself.

It is natural that heavenly reason does not agree with earthly reason.

Reasoning is a ladder; by this ladder one can rise, and from this ladder one may fall.

Reason is a great factor and has all possibility in it of every curse and of every bliss.

Daring is preferred to fearing.

A sparkling soul flashes out through the eyes.

A great person is great with his faults and merits.

Be complete here and perfect there.

A wrong direction may lead to quite the opposite end.

Devotion gives all, asks nothing.

Love knows no limits.

Love keeps back nothing.

If you do not see God in man, you will not see Him anywhere.

You can never be sure of anything in this world of illusion.

If you can no longer love, it proves that you never did love.

The way you choose is the way for you.

Feeling is life and death at the same time.

The eyes are two windows through which the soul looks out.

The benefit of the word Almighty is in its realization.

An infant brings with it the air of heaven on earth.

What is made for man, man may hold; he must not be held by it.

The bringers of joy have always been the children of sorrow.

187

One enemy can do more harm than the good that can be done by a hundred friends.

The virtue of duty is in the pleasure of doing it.

Duty done unwillingly is worse than slavery.

Who else but a noble soul would bear all and say nothing?

By going through sorrow, we rise above it.

The fool fights wisdom wherever he meets it.

By disliking our dislikes, we begin to like all things.

Sympathy robs man of himself.

It is the one who lacks keen observation who becomes critical.

The critical tendency comes from agitation of mind.

Pursuit after the impossible is the best game there is.

The best way to love is to serve.

Some satisfy their vanity by living, others by dying.

Fishers of men have their net of sympathy.

Sensation is a shadow of exaltation.

The world's end comes with the breaking of the heart.

Renounce the world before the world renounces you.

The wicked world does not allow man's fine feelings to be cherished.

When a loving heart manifests jealousy, it is like sweet milk turning sour.

Love creates beauty by her own hands, to worship.

Wisdom is the cream of intelligence.

All learning becomes pale once divine knowledge begins to shine.

A life of superficiality is lived as not lived.

The spirit of man is the egg in which God is formed.

The human heart is the womb from which the Lord is born.

TALAS

THERE is One Individual hidden behind many individuals; there is One Person shining through all personalities.

Loveless is lifeless; loving is living.

One breathes the air of heaven, another goes through the fire of hell; yet both walk on the same earth, both live under the same sun.

There are some who walk, some who creep, some who run, and some who fly; and yet all men are said to be alike.

It is unjust to be rich when others are poor, and it is fatal to be poor when others are rich.

Humility in love is the humility of the master, and humility in surrender is the humility of the slave.

A great person will stretch your mind to the breadth of his own heart, and a small person will narrow it to the size of his own outlook.

There is a right side to every wrong, and a wrong side to every right.

The mind is its question, and it is itself its answer.

All the lack that we find in life is the lack of will, and all the blessing that comes to us comes by the power of will.

The fearing welldoer is worse than a fearless sinner.

If belief is a thing, faith is a living being.

Thoughts have words, feelings have voice, words have forms, voice has soul.

There are some, the closer destiny brings together, the further are their hearts thrown apart; and there are others, the further destiny throws apart, the closer are their hearts brought together.

Sound is the life of life; time is the death of death.

The one who is lost on the path of love is lost for ever; the one who has won on the battlefield of love has won for all eternity.

There is no greater source of pride than a clear conscience; and there is no greater means of humiliation than a guilty conscience.

Sacrifice and renunciation are two things; sacrifice is made by love, renunciation is caused by indifference.

To live means to hope, and to hope means to live.

It takes years to make an ideal, and it takes but a moment to break it.

To love is one thing, and to own is another thing.

The wealth-seeker has no regard for father or brother; the pleasure-seeker considers no honour nor respect; the sorrowful has no comfort nor sleep; the hungry distinguishes not between ripe and unripe.

Do I pass through life? No, it is life that passes by me.

By loving, one melts one's own heart; by possessing, one loads the heart of another.

Possession is self-assertion; loving is self-abnegation. The possessor must lose, sooner or later, the one he possesses; the lover gains in the end, if not the beloved, love itself.

The one who covers his grief under a smile is sincere; the one who covers his laughter under grief is a hypocrite.

Love that depends on being answered by the beloved is lame; it does not stand on its own feet. Love that tries to possess the beloved is without arms; it can never hold. Love that does not regard the pleasure and displeasure of the beloved is blind. Love that is exacting and self-assertive is dead.

The secret of woman's charm is her modesty; the mystery of man's power is his pride.

The lover is blind to the faults of the one he loves, and the hater is blind to the merits of the one he hates.

Wisdom existed before the wise; life existed before the living; love existed before the lover.

The desert can be changed into fertile soil; the land can be changed into the sea; even hell can be changed into heaven; but the mind that is once fixed, cannot be changed.

Words are valuable, but silence is precious.

That which fools can say rudely, the clever cover under a veil; and the wise say the same without saying it.

The day you feel you do not know, you will begin to know.

What is once given is given; what is once done is done; what is once lost is lost; what is once won is won.

Nothing can bind one to another except the thread of sympathy, and nothing can separate one from another except the cutting of that thread.

As eagerly as man is inclined to free himself from a situation, so is he willingly inclined to fall into it.

Nothing is as old as the truth and nothing is as new as the truth.

Make of them big things, if you wish to do small things; and make of them small things, if you wish to do big things.

We speak when we understand the language of one another, and we keep silent when our hearts speak.

Sound is the voice of life; time is the word of death.

There are many sins, small and great; but to recognize sin is the greatest sin.

To step forward is going forward in the path of friendship, and to step backward is going backward.

He who retorts pays the one who insults him, but he who takes silently stands above every insult.

There are two different times in life when the danger of falling awaits man: the time of prosperity and the time of adversity.

All things become wrong when they are not in their right time or when they are not in their proper place.

In order to arrive at spiritual attainment two gulfs must be crossed: the sea of attachment and the ocean of detachment.

There is nothing more subtle or simpler than truth.

Food is the nourishment of the body; thought is a refreshment to the mind; love is the subsistence for the heart; truth is the sustenance of the soul.

Man's ideal shows the height of his heart; man's understanding shows the depth of his heart; man's perception shows the length of his heart; man's sympathy shows the breadth of his heart; but the fourth dimension of man's heart is seen by all that it contains within itself.

Wisdom is different from justice: while justice is expressed in fairness, wisdom is shown by tact.

There are two sorts of persons who show child-like simplicity in their lives: the foolish one, who shows childish traits, and the wise one, who shows the innocence of a child.

There are some who make the dead alive, and there are others who make the living dead.

Two persons are silent on the question of religion: the most foolish and the most wise.

Above law is love; above love is the Beloved.

The power of the word is indeed great, but the power of silence is still greater.

He who speaks much and says little is foolish; he who speaks little and says much is wise.

In the drop, the sea is as small as the drop; in the sea, a drop is as large as the sea.

If it is true, it is as true as false; if it is false, it is as false as true.

He stands above the situation who controls it; he falls beneath the situation who becomes involved in it.

One who looks at life with horror is in the underworld; one who takes life seriously to heart is in the world; the one who smiles at life with a happy smile is above the world.

It is the foolishly selfish who is selfish; the wisely selfish proves to be unselfish.

Before one becomes sharp and the other blunt,
Before one is hot and the other cold,
Before one doubts and the other suspects,

Before one gives up his confidence and the other
    his trust.
It is time that they left one another.

Before one closes his eyes and the other his ears,
Before one turns his head and the other his back,
Before one talks and the other disputes,
Before one is in wrath and the other in rage,
It is time that they left one another.

Friendship, relationship, familiarity, intimacy, all
have their limits; if you go past the limit you
certainly violate the forbidden soil.

There are those who enjoy taking, and there are
those who enjoy giving.

If you can say something without saying, you had
better not say; if you can do something without
doing, you had better not do.

Many live to die, and many die to live.

Even the faults of the meritorious soul become

merits, and even merits of the faulty one turn into faults.

There are two kinds of people: those who are blinded by faith, and those who are blind to faith.

One cannot be real and live in the world of falsehood, and one cannot be false and exist in the world of reality.

Love all, trust none; forgive all, forget none; respect all, worship none. That is the manner of the wise.

The rose brings forth fragrance, colour, and beautiful structure; so the soul, with its unfoldment, shows personality, atmosphere, and refined manner.

The sun, air, water, space, and fertile soil are necessary for the rose to bloom; intelligence, inspiration, love, a wide outlook, and guidance are required for the soul to unfold.

Art without beauty, poetry without inspiration,

music without feeling, science without reason, philosophy without logic, religion without devotion, mysticism without ecstasy are like a lake without water.

A joke without wit, a speech without meaning, tears without romance, learning without wisdom, position without honour, a heart without love, a head without thought are like the space without the air.

A man without manly courage, a woman without womanly grace, a child without a child's simplicity, an infant without an infant's innocence, a lover without willing sacrifice, a worshipper without the ideal of God, a giver without great modesty are like a king without a kingdom.

Criticism, indifference, pessimism are the three things which close the door of the heart.

Love is the object in the life of both devil and saint. The one demands it, the other gives it.

God created man in His own image, and man made God in his own likeness.

What pleasure is there in a useless action?
What interest is there in a senseless speech?
What joy is there in a depthless thought?
What happiness is there in a loveless feeling?

The image of Christ is in the Church, the book of Christ is with the clergy, the love of Christ is in the heart of his worshipper, but the light of Christ shines through the illuminated souls.

GAYATRI

PIR

INSPIRER of my mind, consoler of my
heart, healer of my spirit,
Thy presence lifteth me from earth to heaven,
Thy words flow as the sacred river,
Thy thought riseth as a divine spring,
Thy tender feelings waken sympathy in my
heart.
Beloved Teacher, thy very being is forgiveness.
The clouds of doubt and fear are scattered by
thy piercing glance;
All ignorance vanishes in thy illuminating
presence;
A new hope is born in my heart by breathing
thy peaceful atmosphere.
O inspiring Guide through life's puzzling ways,
In thee I feel abundance of blessing.

NABI

A torch in the darkness, a staff during my
  weakness,
A rock in the weariness of life,
Thou, my Master, makest earth a paradise.
Thy thought giveth me unearthly joy,
Thy light illuminateth my life's path,
Thy words inspire me with divine wisdom,
I follow in thy footsteps, which lead me to
  the eternal goal.
Comforter of the broken-hearted,
Support of those in need,
Friend of the lovers of truth,
Blessed Master, thou art the Prophet of God.

RASUL

Warner of coming dangers,
Wakener of the world from sleep,
Deliverer of the Message of God,
Thou art our Saviour.
The sun at the dawn of creation,
The light of the whole universe,
The fulfilment of God's purpose,
Thou the life eternal, we seek refuge in thy
    loving enfoldment.
Spirit of Guidance, Source of all beauty and
    Creator of harmony,
Love, Lover, and Beloved Lord,
Thou art our divine ideal.

CHALAS

GOD and the devil are the two extreme poles of the ego. One represents perfection, the other limitation.

The moment man realizes when to speak, and when to keep silence, he takes his first step in the path of wisdom.

Living in the world without insight into the hidden laws of nature, is like not knowing the language of the country in which one was born.

A continual pursuit after the impossible is the chronic disease of man.

Seeking after that which is beyond one's reach is the oil which feeds the flame of hope.

The surface of the human intelligence is the

intellect; when it is turned outside in, it becomes the source of all revelation.

Nothing is impossible; all is possible. Impossibility is only a boundary of limitation which stands around the human mind.

Facts lose their colour in the face of truth, as stars pale before the sun.

It is not difficult at all to please the saint; he can most easily be pleased. The difficulty is in pleasing the other, who is the opposite of the saint.

So few in this world discriminate properly between their want and their need.

A responsible person is worth more than a thousand men who labour.

It is true that the light of wisdom must continually be kept alight, but it is difficult always to act rightly.

Either you must pass from all things that interest you in this life, or else they will pass you; for the nature of this unstable life is changing.

Through every condition, agreeable or disagreeable, the soul makes its way towards the goal.

The lover who leans upon the beloved's response, his love is like the flame that needs oil to live; but the lover who stands on his own feet, is like the lantern of the sun that burns without oil.

A simple statement often takes away the charm of something which may be left unsaid.

If people do not come up to your mark, do not become annoyed, but rejoice, knowing that your mark is high.

The sense of discretion is instinctive, and it is the life one lives that either shapes or deforms it.

There is no gain without sacrifice; if there be any, sacrifice must follow.

Are you looking for an ideal soul? Such a person has never been born. But if you still seek after him, then you will have to create one of your own imagination.

When you have learned all there is to be learned, then you will realize that there was nothing to be learned.

The moment a prisoner feels that he will no longer remain in the prison, the prison bars must break instantly, of themselves.

Contentment raises man above the strife of worthless things and beyond the limitation of human nature.

It is seldom that too little is said and too much is done, but often the contrary.

The motive power is creative and constructive, yet it is motive that limits the power which is limitless.

All pain is significant of change; all that changes for

better or worse must cause a certain amount of pain, for change is at once birth and death.

All conventionality, that has limited the life of man and has removed it far from nature, comes from sex distinction.

Man was sent into the artificial world that he might meet every conventionality, in which lies all tragedy of life.

One who lacks imagination, and is of little faith, is unable to tread the spiritual path.

Faith and imagination are wings of the bird that flies in the spiritual spheres.

If the owl of Sophia had been as wise as she, it would not have sat in her presence so spellbound.

Kindness which is not balanced with firmness may prove to be weakness.

People are not only ready to profit by your

wisdom, power, and greatness, but they are also eager to take advantage of your ignorance, weakness, and inability.

Being able to trust others apart, if you have learned to trust yourself, you have accomplished something.

Every person has a place in life, and no one can hold a place long that is not his own.

By trying to look upon life not only from one's own point of view but also from the point of view of another, one loses nothing, but on the contrary widens the horizon of one's view.

To express an impulse gives relief, but to control it gives strength.

Perfection is attained by five achievements: life, light, power, happiness, and peace.

By creating happiness, one fulfils one's life's purpose.

If dogs bark at the elephant, it takes no notice and goes on its way; so do the wise when attacked by the ignorant.

There are many wrong paths, but there is one right way that leads to the goal.

You will find reasons, whether you want to be pessimistic or optimistic, to support your view.

The seer distinguishes between the real and the unreal, until he arrives at a point where all to him becomes the reality.

When you do not concern yourself with the consequences, then alone you may freely express your impulse.

One cannot be wise and foolish at the same time, for light and darkness cannot dwell together.

Illuminated souls do not seek after occult powers; but occult powers, by themselves, come to them.

It is not the heart of earth in which to confide, for it brings forth all that is given to it in simple trust; it is the soul of heaven which is trustworthy, for it assimilates all in its own being.

Why? is an animal with a thousand tails. At every bite you give it, it drops one of its curved tails and raises another. Its hunger is never satisfied so long as its mouth is open.

Life is the longing of every soul; the one who seeks life through death becomes immortal.

Those whom you have lost here, you will find in some other place.

In the friendship, as well as in the hostility of the worldly, there is pain.

'Yesterday I was not wise enough, today I understand, tomorrow I will do better!' So man thinks and life goes on.

The prophet is the painter of that ideal which is beyond man's comprehension.

What does it matter if Krishna was Christ, or Brahma was Abraham? One thing is true: that there was, there is, and there always will be a knower of God, a lover of souls, a server of humanity.

The man who tries to prove his belief superior to the faith of another, does not know the meaning of religion.

When a person argues on a problem, it does not always mean that he knows it. Most often he argues because he wants to complete his knowledge without admitting his ignorance.

The light illuminates the path of those who are distant from it; those who are near are dazzled by it.

There can be no comparison between art and nature; for art is as limited as man, but nature is as perfect as God.

Self-effacement does not in any way lessen; it only makes one limitless.

Duty is not necessarily the purpose of life; still, in duty one finds a road which leads one to the purpose of life.

No sooner is the God-ideal brought to life than the worshipper of God turns into truth. Then truth is no longer his seeking; truth becomes his being; and in the light of that absolute truth he finds all knowledge.

It was not the Lord who was crucified, it was his limitation.

If an idol made of rock is made God by its worshippers, why then should a personality not become Divinity for the devotees?

The one who makes fun of another, seldom knows that there is something laughable in himself also.

Every man has his own reason; therefore two persons cannot always understand each other.

There is one thing to be said against the kind-hearted: that they never can be kind enough.

Whether a small person loves you or hates you, in either case he will pull you down to his own level.

To delve into a matter which matters little, is like raising dust from the ground.

It is belief which in its perfection becomes faith.

Even a plain thought gets tangled when told to a person who has a knot in his head.

When a thoughtful person risks falling at each step he takes in the path of life, what about a thoughtless person?

Despair not if your friend has taken advantage of you, but be contented, knowing that it was not your enemy.

There are habits which can best be prevented

before one has formed them. Once you have taken to a habit, then it is difficult to give it up.

Rules of the world are different from the law of the path that the mystics tread.

He who fights for justice in the affairs of this world, may fight for ever, for he will never find it; justice is only manifest in the sum total of life.

When you stand on this earth and look at life, there is all injustice and chaos everywhere; but when you rise above and look below, it is all just and perfect, and everything appears to be in its proper place.

When man arrives at God-knowledge from self-knowledge, he makes God as small as his little self; but when he comes to self-knowledge through the knowledge of God, he becomes as large as God.

The supreme law is that all is just and all is right. But is this law to be proclaimed? No, it is to be understood.

The attribute is not important; it is the possessor of the attribute who is important.

If someone can discover, with any authority, the true source of happiness, he can find it only in pain.

Faith is the culmination of belief. It is that faith which is the mystery of life, the secret of salvation.

It is not evidence which gives belief. Belief which stands above evidences is that belief which, in the end, will culminate in faith.

Belief is the food of the believer; it is the sustenance of his faith. It is on belief he lives, not on food and water.

By learning to think, one develops dignity in nature. The more one thinks, the more dignified one becomes; because dignity springs out of thoughtfulness.

Reason belongs both to earth and heaven. Its depth

is heavenly, its surface earthly; and that which fills the gap in the form of reason, between heaven and earth, is that middle part of it which unites it. Therefore reason can be most confusing and reason can be most enlightening.

The reason why man seeks for happiness is not because happiness is his sustenance, but because happiness is his own being; therefore, in seeking for happiness, man is seeking for himself.

Religion is not in performing a ceremony or a ritual; true religion is the feeling, or the sense, of duty.

Woman, whom destiny has made to be man's superior, by trying to become his equal, falls beneath his estimation.

What virtue is that, O righteous man, which gives no happiness?

If you have lost something, it means that you have either risen above it or fallen below it.

Man expects another to place him in a higher position, but the place to which he is equal, he takes himself.

The dead can give nothing living, nor can the living give anything dead.

It is better that your enemy stands before your house rather than that he should live under your roof.

White forces or dark forces, all will surrender to you with the waxing of the moon of your life; but in the waning moon they will show their influence.

It matters little whether you are on the top of the mountain or at the foot of it, if you are happy where you are.

If you feel your thoughts, your thoughts will become your being.

The one who is not moved to dance by the movements of an innocent babe, has not yet risen from his grave.

One cannot praise God unless one makes of Him an ideal.

Watching with interest the winning ways of a little child, is a wonderful love-making.

Every thing and every being is placed in its own place in life, and each is busy carrying out that work which has to be done in the whole scheme of nature.

A religious ritual, for a spiritual person, is but a recreation.

To find appropriate words to express an idea is more complicated than painting a picture.

Destiny can take your best friend as an instrument

to cause you harm, and your worst enemy to do you good.

Power is utilized to its best advantage when it is used for a good purpose.

If one lacks understanding, one is poor with all the goods of the world one possesses; it is understanding which is the true riches.

The man who complains about everything certainly has a complaint somewhere in his head.

Sensation and exaltation are two things: pleasure comes from sensation, happiness from exaltation.

No sooner do you begin to see the bad side of man's character than you automatically throw a cover over the good side of his nature.

Man, however great, must not claim perfection; for the blind world can only see the limitation of his external being.

There are some souls who, if you do not make them your friends, will become your enemies.

The one who wants to become a master must first pass through an examination as a servant.

God cannot be good and perfect at the same time; it takes good and bad both to make perfection.

Fools are not entitled to know the mystery which the wise are supposed to possess.

The knowledge of truth does not suffice for imparting it to others; one must know the psychology of human nature.

The purpose of life is fulfilled in rising to the greatest heights and in diving to the deepest depths of life.

Peace will not come to a lover's heart so long as he will not become love itself.

All things pertaining to spiritual progress in life depend upon peace.

The most beautiful form of the love of God is His compassion, His divine forgiveness.

NIRTAN

CONTENTS

229

ALANKARAS

THOU changest thy place, but not thyself, O Light.

Unfold Thy secret through nature, and reveal Thy mystery through my heart.

Thou art my spirit, I am Thy body, my Holy One.

Let the sun of Thy divine spirit rise from my heart, that morning may break out of the darkness of life.

I shall penetrate through the black heart of the clouds to reach Thee, my Lord.

My life is a wave of the ocean of Thy eternal life.

Let my soul become Thy life.

Through the darkness of night my soul seeks for Thee.

Waken me, Lord, through Thy Warner, while I am asleep in the arms of error.

It is Thy spirit of Risalat which is divinity.

Thine own desire I see fulfilled, O God, in the perfection of Rasul.

I hold an ear to the depth of Thy blessing when the storm breaks through life's sea.

Let me recognize Thy divine visage in the image of Thy Message-bearer.

My heart is no more mine, it is thine own, my spiritual Guide.

Heal my soul by the all-sufficient power that comes from the glance of Thy Messiah.

O, your rising waves of favour,
And your raging flames of wrath!
On the rose they are like dew-drops,
On the flame just like the moth.

My spiritual Guide, thou bearest in thyself the spirit of Rasul.

The dark clouds brought romance between Thee, my Beloved, and me.

Let my heart reflect the spirit of the Holy Ones.

Let my self turn into Thy being.

My vanity! It amuses me to see thee dance at the sight of my limitation.

The rapture of my heart shows the mark of Thy kiss.

Let Thy perfection be mine, and my imperfection be cleared away as the mist in the sun.

My heart! At times one moment is as a year, and at times one year is as a moment to thee.

I cry and shed tears when clouds gather round

my heart, and when the light of my soul is covered from my sight.

Mother's arms receive me when I come to the earth; Father's arms lift me up at the moment when I depart hence.

HEART

The heart has its head on its own palm,
The face of the heart is veiled;
The heart's hands are bound with iron chains,
The feet of the heart are nailed.

The eyes of the heart are never dry,
The heart speaks only through tears.
The ears of the heart are so keen
That the voice from a distance it hears.

The voice of the heart is silent,
Yet far-reaching is heart's cry.
The heart has no question nor answer,
The heart is expressed in a sigh.

The ways of the heart are mysterious,
The heart has the mind of a child.
The heart's breath is full of tenderness,
The heart's expression is mild.

The ideal alone is heart's deity,
A constant yearning its life.
The heart's not concerned with life or death,
The heart stands firm through all strife.

Beauty is heart's only object,
Its inspirer, its all.
The heart is all power that there is,
The angels attend its call.

The heart is itself its own medicine,
The heart all its own wounds heals.
And none can ever imagine
The pain that the loving heart feels.

The path of the heart is thorny,
But leads in the end to bliss.
Hope is the staff the heart holds in hand,
And the goal heart shall not miss.

TRUTH

The face of truth is open,
The eyes of truth are bright,
The lips of truth are ever closed,
The head of truth is upright.
The breast of truth stands forward,
The gaze of truth is straight,
Truth has neither fear nor doubt,
Truth has patience to wait.
The words of truth are touching,
The voice of truth is deep,
The law of truth is simple:
All that you sow you reap.
The soul of truth is flaming,
The heart of truth is warm,
The mind of truth is clear,
And firm through rain or storm.
Facts are but its shadows,
Truth stands above all sin;
Great be the battle in life,
Truth in the end shall win.

The image of truth is Christ,
Wisdom's message its rod;
Sign of truth is the cross,
Soul of truth is God.
Life of truth is eternal,
Immortal is its past,
Power of truth will endure,
Truth shall hold to the last.

SURAS

THERE is no reason that man should know God because he is born on earth; it is only the birth of his soul that makes him entitled to that knowledge.

Life is reality, death is its shadow; but as the shadow is seen and yet non-existent, so is death.

Death opens a door between life here and hereafter.

Death is a silent voyage to the port of eternity.

Death is no more death to those who have once experienced its sting.

Death is but the turning of a page of life; to the eyes of others it is death, but to those who die it is life.

TANAS

GLORIOUS sun, are you setting?
— Yes, to rise again.

Sublime nature, my ears did not hear your music.
— Your heart has heard it, your soul has danced
to it.

Trees to the clouds:—With raised hands we pay
you our homage.
Clouds:—In tears we grant your request.

Nature, where do you borrow your sublimity?
— From your loving spirit.

Rain, why do you not come in the desert?
— I keep away from where I am not welcome.

When once passing through the mountains, I saw
rocks, some resting on their knees, some bending,
some standing. I asked, 'O hard-hearted monsters,

what secret is there in your charm?' They answered in a silent voice, 'That we do not assert ourselves'.

Rocky mountains, what are you?
— We are the tombs of the world's past.

Crystal, what are you?
— I am the shadow of Christ's heart.
What quality do you possess?
— I am empty of self, so that by gazing, one sees in me His heart reflected.

Desert to the rain-clouds:—You are passing over us, why not be our guest?
Rain-clouds:—We have no longer trust in the hard-hearted.

Glorious nature, wonderful picture, where shall I keep you?
— In the frame of your heart.

Wilderness, why does your cry touch me so deeply?
— Because it rises from the bottom of my heart.

Wilderness, what is in you that is so overwhelming?
— The expansion of my heart.

Good-bye, nature's vision, shall I ever see you again?
— Yes, whenever you open the album of your heart.

GAMAKAS

WHY was I born, O God, if not to find Thee?
Why do I die, O God, if not to come to Thee?

When the unreality of life pushes against my heart,
its door opens to the reality.

The past was my dream, the present is my play,
and the future will be my plan.

I reach Thee before my feet can reach Thy
dwelling-place, and I see Thee before mine eyes
can reach Thy spheres.

I was perfected by heaven, but am limited by the
earth.

Can anyone break me? No. By doing so, he may
as well prepare to break God. Neither I nor God
can be broken; but the one who would wish to
break me, he is broken.

I draw all my strength from my humility.

A tongue of flame rises from every wound of my heart, illuminating my path through life and guiding my way to the goal.

The rapidity of my walk the imagination cannot follow.

People often ask me questions which I cannot very well answer in words, and it makes me sad to think they are unable to hear the voice of my silence.

By every hurt or harm one causes me, he only makes me know him better.

I came as I was made to come; I live as life allows me to live; but I will be what I wish to be.

With every pinprick a drop of blood comes out of my heart, and that drop becomes the Wine of Sacrament.

I have not come to teach those who consider themselves teachers; I have come to learn from the teachers and to teach my pupils.

When my heart is perturbed it upsets the whole universe.

When my heart is asleep, then both worlds fall into a deep slumber.

The whole creation wakes up with the wakening of my heart.

When the shell of my heart breaks, pearls are scattered around.

My heart attains self-sufficiency by eating its own flesh and by drinking its own blood.

I tremble at the sight of the task that has been given to me, and I feel confounded when I weigh my ideal with my limitations.

What the world calls success, is to me like a dolls' wedding.

I am the Wine of the Holy Sacrament; my very being is intoxication; those who drink of my cup and yet keep sober will certainly be illuminated; but those who do not assimilate it, will be beside themselves and exposed to the ridicule of the world.

My heart drinks its own tears and puts them forth as pearls.

I prefer failure to success gained by falsehood.

I am what I am; you make me what you will make me; but I become what I wish to become.

The true exaltation comes to me from the insults I have to endure in life rather than from the respectful attitude of my mureeds.

Many underestimate the greatness of the Cause, seeing the limitation through which I have to work my way out.

The Message is a call to those whose hour has come

to awake, and it is a lullably to those who are still meant to sleep.

How can a man claim to be a teacher and at the same time be sane? His teaching must prove him a teacher, not his claim.

The essence of today's Message is balance.

You are my life, it is in you that I live,
From you I borrow life and you do I give;
O my soul and spirit, you I adore,
I live in you, so do I live ever more.
You are in me and in you do I live,
Still you are my King and my sins you forgive.
You are the Present and Future and Past;
I lost myself, but I have found you at last.

Why, O my feeling heart
    Do you live and die?
What makes my feeling heart
    To laugh and to cry?
Death is my life indeed;
    I live when I die.
Pain is my pleasure; when
    I laugh, then I cry.

Some did say that I knew nothing,
Some still held that I knew all.
Some did turn their back to me, and
Some quickly answered my call.
Some on hearing my words exclaimed,
'Nothing he said that was new'.
Some said, 'I have always thought this;
That is my own point of view'.
Some asked, 'What mystery he revealed?
What wonder did he perform?'
Some answered, 'We ask no wonder,
So long as his heart is warm'.
Some said, 'He is a man as we are,
What difference in him do you see?'
Some answered, 'It is not to *know*;
What is needed, is to *be*'.

Before you judge my actions,
Lord, I pray, you will forgive.
Before my heart has broken,
Will you help my soul to live?
Before my eyes are covered,
Will you let me see your face?
Before my feet are tired,
May I reach your dwelling-place?

Before I wake from slumber,
You will watch me, Lord, I hold.
Before I throw my mantle,
Will you take me in your fold?
Before my work is over,
You, my Lord, will right the wrong.
Before you play your music,
Will you let me sing my song?

BOULAS

THE saints are forgiveness itself.

In the influence that controls a situation the hand of God is seen.

The more one can bear, the more one is given to bear.

If one wants to know life, one can best know it by one's own life.

No beloved has ever known the depth of the lover's heart.

Sometimes success is a defeat and defeat is a success.

The greater the responsibility, the greater the person.

Man unconsciously pays happiness in order to buy pleasure.

Life is interesting with friends and enemies both.

A sharp tongue can cut one deeper than a knife.

Sin is a sin, whether thought, said, or done.

There are many dead sins, but to separate two loving hearts is a living sin.

Every difficulty can be made easy by the power of a willing spirit.

Man sees in another his own fault.

Give not nor claim love by force, for love is an affair of mutual willingness.

Silence is an unadmitting consent and an uncommitting refusal.

Walking on the turning wheel of the earth, living

under the ever-rotating sun, man expects a peaceful life.

Man's jealousy is woman's vanity.

A consent after refusing is worse than a refusal.

To discover the heart is the greatest initiation.

One's own self has the right to accuse oneself of one's faults, rather than anyone else.

Truth is born of falsehood as light comes from darkness.

A charming personality is great riches.

The mysic perfects himself by making himself empty of himself.

Sorrow enables man to experience joy.

The punishment of the God of Compassion is a reward too.

The Creator, by means of the human heart, experiences life within and without.

Tears of joy are more precious than pearls.

If you avoid wrongdoing, it will avoid you.

A real artist expresses his soul in his art.

Divinity is the exaltation of the human soul.

It is not the action which is a sin; it is the attitude of mind which makes it so.

Silence speaks louder than words.

Reality unfolds with the breaking of the heart.

The vision of nature is the presence of God.

In the heart of sorrow there is a seed of joy.

A sharp tongue is a poisoned sword.

A house is built with matter, but made with spirit.

The one who troubles much about the cause is far removed from the cause.

Righteousness gives strength, and falseness weakens the mind.

No one would do wrong if he knew the wrong of it.

Love in giving and taking is commercialized. In its pure essence love is for its own joy.

The spirit of feeling is lost when a sentiment is expressed in words.

No earth, no water, no fire, no air can ever disunite two hearts that have become one.

Retire from the mundane things of life as much as life will permit you.

Avoid all nonsense.

Accomplishment is more valuable than what is accomplished.

Life is time, and death is its division.

We need not tolerate inharmony, but we can act indifference to it.

Evil is like a shadow.

He who gives love will receive a thousandfold in return.

It is the separation which is separated, not we.

Nature is born, character is built, and personality is developed.

Time and space are the hands and feet of the mystic; through space he climbs, and through time he accomplishes.

The same thing that may bring pride to one, may cause shame to another.

Man seeks freedom and pursues captivity.

The one who seeks the spiritual path is sought after by the spirit.

To life there is no death, and to death there is no life.

Perfection is to be found in looking for One, in pursuing One, in finding One, in realizing One.

The more you depend upon God, the more God becomes dependable.

Love's reward is love itself.

The essence of reason is the knowledge of God.

TALAS

BEFOOL not, O night, the morn will break; beware, O darkness, the sun will shine; be not vain, O mist, it will once more be clear; my sorrow, forget not, once again joy will arise.

A labour done without wages, a service without thanks, a merit without appreciation, a love without answer have a different value.

It is a weakness to withdraw from struggle; it is foolishness to go through it.

If you are annoyed by any disagreeable experience, it is a loss; but if you have learnt by it, it is a gain.

What feeling it is to ask forgiveness to those who must ask forgiveness of you, and to thank those who must thank you!

It does not matter how hard you labour; it is what you accomplish that counts.

Wickedness that manifests from an intelligent person is like a poisonous fruit springing from a fertile ground.

The life of love is more than innumerable lives, and the death of love is worse than a thousand deaths.

As the birds will never have a lasting attachment to beasts, so it is even with man: the wayfarer of the heavens can never keep constantly attached to the dweller of the earth.

Knowledge ends in no knowledge, learning ends in unlearning.

Sweeter than honey are the results of one's toil; more fragrant than flowers are the words of praise; more delicious than fruit is an obedient child; more precious than a pearl is a congenial mate.

A beautiful sin is a virtue, and an ugly virtue is a sin.

Impulse is intoxicating; action is absorbing; but it is the result of every deed that leads man to realization.

An optimist takes the chance of losing; a pessimist loses the chance of gaining.

When you care for the opinion of others, you are below them; when you do not care, you are above them.

It is the lover's heart that touches the depths of life; it is the godly soul that soars to the highest heavens; it is the seer's eye that penetrates through the wall of matter; and it is the knower's spirit that assimilates all the knowledge.

We experience death by playing life, and we experience life by playing death.

CHALAS

IF a man of principle makes a breach of law, it is to pursue a high ideal.

Raise not dust from the ground; it will enter into your eyes. Sprinkle some water on it that it may settle down and lie under your feet.

A wrongdoer who is sorry for his wrongdoings profits more than the one who has never done wrong.

It does not need courage to be bold and blunt, sharp and rude; one has only to be shameless.

Pick not flowers, for it will detain you in your progress on the path, and as you go, they will only fade away. Look at them therefore and admire their beauty, and as you proceed on your journey, they will greet you with smiles all along the way.

THE SUFI MESSAGE OF HAZRAT INAYAT KHAN
VOLS I-XIII + INDEX

Volume I. *The Way of Illumination*
The traditional Sufic outlook of life's values and purpose
is re-expressed by Hazrat Inayat Khan in universal and
contemporary concepts. Included are: *The Way of Illumination; The Inner Life; The Soul; Whence and Whither* and *The
Purpose of Life.*

Volume II. *The Mysticism of Music, Sound and Word*
Sufism traditionally used music as a means of transmitting
the essence of mystical insight. Hazrat Inayat Khan inte-
grates this concept of music with elements like sound and
silence, vibration and the word, thoughts and inspiration,
creating new dimensions for our lives, and thereby
recomposing a musical concept extending beyond the
tradition of time and culture.

Volume III. *The Art of Personality*
This volume contains the substances of Hazrat Inayat
Khan's teaching on our Divine heritage and human rela-
tionships, including the science of life's forces. He suggests

that the art of personality is the completion of nature and the culmination of heredity. Development of the personality is taken from before birth to the deepest aspects of consciousness.

Included are: *Education; Rasa Shastra; Character-Building and the Art of Personality; Moral Culture.*

Volume IV. *Mental Purification and Healing*

In this volume the Sufi principles are explained concerning the influence the mind may exert on the body, in relation to the spiritual power within us, and concerning the possibilities of spiritual healing in conjunction with modern science.

Included are: *Health; Mental Purification; The Mind World.*

Volume V. *Spiritual Liberty*

This volume contains a wealth of information about different aspects of Sufi mysticism.

Included are: *A Sufi Message of Spiritual Liberty: Aqibat: Life and Death; The Phenomenon of the Soul; Love, Human and Divine; Pearls from the Ocean Unseen.*

Volume VI. *The Alchemy of Happiness*

Hazrat Inayat Khan always insisted that spiritual or mystical aspirations are of no avail if one's life is not lived as it should be. Under this title, forty lectures are collected that deal with life in all its aspects.

Volume VII. *In an Eastern Rose Garden*
Talks given by Hazrat Inayat Khan on a variety of subjects.
His ability to communicate the unity and relativity of his
viewpoint on diverse subjects illustrates the essence of his
mystical perception of life.

Volume VIII. *Sufi Teachings*
A collection of talks on various practical and esoteric
aspects of traditional Sufi teachings developed by Hazrat
Inayat Khan in a modern and universal context.

Volume IX. *The Unity of Religious Ideals*
A systematically arranged collection of Hazrat Inayat
Khan's addresses on what is perhaps the most important
part of his teaching: the underlying unity of all religious
thought and experience.

Volume X. *Sufi Mysticism*
Hazrat Inayat Khan situates the traditional concepts of
initiation, discipleship, spiritual teaching and other esoteric aspects of Sufism in today's world. Besides the main
part consisting of: *Sufi Mysticism* and *The Path of Initiation
and Discipleship*, these subjects are included: *Sufi Poetry;
Art: Yesterday, Today and Tomorrow; The Problem of the Day.*

Volume XI. *Philosophy, Psychology, Mysticism*
These later talks by Hazrat Inayat Khan, given during the
last two years before his death, contain a clear overview of
these topics in terms of his Sufic vision. This series of
lectures may be considered his *magnum opus*. The Apho-

risms at the end are sayings noted down by his pupils which Hazrat Inayat Khan expressed at different times and places to soothe or clarify the seeker.

Volume XII. *The Divinity of the Human Soul*
The first part of this volume deals with the relationship of man and God. The second part is autobiographical. The third part contains four short plays written by Hazrat Inayat Khan for his pupils.
Included are: *The Vision of God and Man; Confessions; Four Plays*

Volume XIII. *Sacred Readings: The Gatha's*
This volume contains the teachings derived from classes given by Hazrat Inayat Khan to his pupils at the earlier stages of their training.

Volume XIV. *Index to Volumes I-XIII.*
This volume is published for the first time. It will be of great interest for the student of Sufism.

The above volumes have been published by MOTILAL BANARSIDASS PUBLISHERS PVT. LTD., Delhi during 1988-1990 and are available in separate volumes or in a set.

Sufi Hazrat Inayat Khan was born in Baroda on July 5th, 1882. His father, Mashaik Rahmat Khan, was descended from Pir Jammashah. His mother, Begum Khadija, came from a Zamindar family of Mysore. He studied music at the Gayan Shala musical academy in Baroda (founded by his grandfather, Maula Bhaksh, court musician of the Maharaja of Baroda). He travelled throughout India and became very well known as a court singer and Saraswati Veena player. He was initiated in the Chishtia and Qadria Sufi Orders by Syed Abu Hashim Madani of Hyderabad and in his travels he studied the religious and mystical Orders of India.

At the age of 28, he left for the West with his brothers Mahboob Khan, Ali Khan and Musharaff Khan. Between 1910 and the twenties they performed music in the great concert halls of Europe and America, being the first professional group to present both Hindustani and Karnatic music to the West. Hazrat Inayat Khan, later succeeded by his brothers, founded the Sufi Movement. He delivered the Sufi Message of Love, Harmony and Beauty, amongst others through lectures which now are being published in India for the first time. He passed away on February 5th, 1927 in New Delhi.